PROFESSIONALISM AND FLEXIBILITY
FOR LEARNING

PROFESSIONALISM AND FLEXIBILITY IN LEARNING

Donald Bligh
(Editor)

Richard Hoggart   Michael Stephens   John Taylor
and   Richard Smethurst
Sinclair Goodlad   and   Brian Pippard
Lewis Elton
Paul Black   and   John Sparkes

SOCIETY FOR RESEARCH INTO HIGHER EDUCATION

Research into Higher Education Monographs

The Society for Research into Higher Education,
At the University, Guildford, Surrey GU2 5XH

First published 1982

© 1982 Society for Research into Higher Education

ISBN 0 900868 87 2

Printed in England by Direct Design (Bournemouth) Ltd. Printers
Butts Pond Industrial Estate, Sturminster Newton,
Dorset DT10 1AZ

THE LEVERHULME PROGRAMME
OF
STUDY INTO THE FUTURE OF HIGHER EDUCATION

This is the sixth publication of a programme of study focusing informed opinion and recent research findings on the major strategic options likely to be available to higher education institutions and policy-making bodies in the 1980s and 1990s. The programme as a whole has been made possible by a generous grant from the Leverhulme Trust to the Society for Research into Higher Education and is entirely independent of governmental or other organizational pressure. The present monograph is the first of two arising out of a specialist seminar on the teaching function in higher education. We are extremely grateful to Sir Bruce Williams, Director of the Technical Change Centre, for his excellent chairmanship as well as for his considerable interest in the whole programme.

A fundamental question facing higher education is the extent to which consensual arrangements and assumptions that generally worked well during the long postwar period of its expansion can cope with the much more stringent conditions likely to prevail in the 1980s and 1990s. Is there sufficient common purpose amongst the various institutions and interest groups that constitute 'the higher education system' to permit the development of viable long-run policy objectives, or must higher education policy increasingly become merely the outcome of a struggle for survival and dominance among conflicting interests and ideas?

This is both a substantive and a methodological question. Substantively it will be faced squarely in the final report of the programme of study. Methodologically it will be tackled in the way the conclusions of that final report are reached.

In brief, the study is an experiment in formulating long-term strategies openly, taking into account the best available specialist knowledge about a complex system, the legitimate interests of a wide range of conflicting pressure groups, and wider public interests as perceived by disinterested individuals with no direct day-to-day involvement in higher education. The final recommendations will be the result of an iterative process in which proposals are made, then discussed, then revised, then reconsidered. Stage One is to commission research reviews by acknowledged experts in various specialist areas. Stage Two is a seminar at which others with detailed knowledge and experience of the area discuss these reviews. Stage Three is publication of the reviews together with a report of the discussion and of the policy implications highlighted by it. Stage Four is wider debate in the press and in specially convened conferences. Stage Five is reconsideration of the policy issues in the light of the wider reaction. Stage Six is the preparation of a final report. A seventh stage is of course hoped for, in which public authorities and institutions of higher education will take up the report's recommendations.

Publication of this monograph, together with its successor, the seventh in the SRHE Leverhulme series, represents the conclusion of the first three stages in that part of the programme concerned with the teaching function in higher education.

Other volumes in the series dealt with higher education and the labour market, access to higher education, institutional change in higher education, the future of research, and the arts and higher education.

The reports on all the seminars, together with comments on them from interested organizations and individuals, will form the basis for a final report setting out the conclusions and policy recommendations of the programme as a whole. This will be drawn up by the chairmen of the seminars and the editors of the accompanying monographs under the chairmanship of Lord Scarman and will be published in June 1983.

The scope of the Leverhulme programme is very wide. The need for a major review of higher education has been recognized by informal commentators for some time, and the financial stringency of recent years has made this need even more apparent. In its report *The Funding and Organisation of Courses in Higher Education* the Education, Science and Arts Committee of the House of Commons commended the SRHE Leverhulme programme of study, and concluded, 'We believe that higher education is at a watershed in its development and that the time is ripe for a great national debate....' The SRHE Leverhulme programme is intended to contribute to that debate by offering both a structure within which the main issues can be considered and an assessment of the evidence on which future policy should be based.

Gareth Williams
Programme Director

FOREWORD

by Sir Bruce Williams

The SRHE Leverhulme seminar on the teaching function in higher education institutions — the sixth in the series — discussed problems of teaching, learning and examining. In recent years there has been considerable criticism of staff performance in teaching and examining and of student performance in learning. There has also been a keener research interest in the three activities and, indeed, some of the criticism has arisen from that research.

Teaching performance has been criticized on the grounds that teachers (or some, or many, of them) are unclear or misguided about objectives, and do not give sufficient thought to the learning processes of students. In the case of universities a further complaint is often heard — namely that the postwar growth of emphasis on research has led to a contraction of interest in teaching undergraduates.

Although criticism of examining is not new, the extent of criticism has increased. There are criticisms that students vary in their response to different forms of exams, that different examiners often give very different marks, that many examiners cannot give a clear account of what they are trying to test, and that what should be tested cannot be summed up adequately in one number or letter. As judged by the extent of change in methods of examining in the past fifteen years, these criticisms have been taken more seriously by staff. But this response to criticism has induced a further criticism that not enough has been done to test the efficacy of the new methods.

Criticism of the performance of the students' learning may be directed at the students for lack of motivation or knowhow, or at the staff for failing to motivate them (or to give appropriate tests of entry) or to provide adequate opportunities to acquire the knowhow. These are fields in which criticism is easy to make and in one sense to justify. But despite a considerable amount of research into the learning process our understanding of it is far from complete, and that is an indication of the difficulties involved in improving performance.

However, it is reasonable to assume that the process of teaching, learning and examining can be improved, and the seminar papers published in the sixth and seventh volumes of the SRHE Leverhulme series contain some important proposals for reform.

Most academics have highly developed critical capacities, though the balance between their critical activities directed inwards and outwards is not always optimal. But when they do get down to critizing teaching and examining activities they can be very fierce — at the seminar there were several occasions when I thought it right to protest that there was some very good teaching and examining, that there were some very good examples of well considered new approaches to teaching and examining in which care had been taken to provide for a running appraisal, and there was some very effective learning.

It would be wrong to give the impression that there are generally grave deficiencies in teaching, examining and learning. Doubtless there is room for improvement, and I hope that these SRHE Leverhulme volumes will stimulate improvements.

Bruce Williams
Chairman

CONTENTS

INTRODUCTION AND ACKNOWLEDGEMENTS 7

SEMINAR PARTICIPANTS 10

1 RECOMMENDATIONS FOR LEARNING 11
  by Donald Bligh

  The need for more professionalism — The need
  for more flexibility — Conclusion

2 CONTINUING EDUCATION WITHIN UNIVERSITIES 31
  AND POLYTECHNICS
  *by Richard Hoggart, Michael Stephens, John Taylor
  and Richard Smethurst*

  Introduction — Why emphasize education for
  adults? — Staff and students: attitudes and
  demands — What should be done? — Examples
  of recent developments — Conclusion

3 THE CURRICULUM OF HIGHER EDUCATION 68
  *by Sinclair Goodlad and Brian Pippard with
  Donald Bligh*

  Summary — Introduction — Professionalism
  and a sense of purpose — Activity for learning
  — The flexibility of general and specialist
  courses — Professional standards and assessment —
  Towards professional flexibility

4 ASSESSMENT FOR LEARNING 106
  by Lewis Elton

  Introduction — Purposes of assessment —
  Assessment as a measuring instrument — Assessment
  and curricular aims — Methods of assessment —
  Assessment schemes — Marking, interpreting,
  reporting — The management of assessment —
  Assessment and 'real life' — Conclusion

5 TEACHING AND LEARNING 136
by Paul Black and John Sparkes

Introduction — Students — Academic staff as professional teachers — Educational systems

INTRODUCTION AND ACKNOWLEDGEMENTS

INTRODUCTION

Educational policies, whether they are national, institutional or departmental, come from somewhere. They reflect, and are formed within, a climate of opinions. The overall purpose of the SRHE Leverhulme Programme of Study into the Future of Higher Education is to contribute to that climate by informed debate and publications.

This book, the sixth report of the programme of study, presents the recommendations of, and some of the papers presented to, the programme's seminar on the teaching function. The remaining papers appear in *Accountability or Freedom for Teachers?*, the seventh report in the series.

It is fairly evident that the field of the seminar was enormous. Although it lasted three and a half days and was the longest in the SRHE Leverhulme programme, we could not expect to cover the whole field.

The Consultative Method
Partly because of the size of the field and partly because the aim of the SRHE Leverhulme programme was to stimulate debate, I tried to pursue a widely consultative method. There was another reason. While the topics of some of the other seminars have been highly specialized (eg the labour market), most students and teachers in higher education believe they have worthwhile opinions about teaching, and they have differing opinions which cannot always be resolved by researchers or other 'experts'.

Topics were selected after consultation with people respected for their wisdom and experience in higher education. To advance our discussions authors were asked to present issues or recommendations (neutrally called 'propositions'). In this they were encouraged to be radical, or at least to take risks, rather than to be academically cautious.

Issues and recommendations contained in the first drafts of the papers, and in some cases the drafts themselves, were made available to five 'pre-seminars' held at Manchester, Strathclyde, Bristol, Leeds and London. Proceedings from the pre-seminars at Manchester and Bristol have been published by SCEDSIP (Standing Conference on Educational Development Services in Polytechnics) under the titles *Course Evaluation and the Teaching Function* and *Three Ways to Learn*.

The Recommendations
Authors have modified their papers to take account of points raised at the pre-seminars and the main seminar itself. In this volume the recommendations of authors are gathered at the beginning of each chapter and in most cases they provide a quick overview for readers who may wish to proceed more selectively.

Towards the end of the main seminar, participants were asked to submit ten recommendations to me, ensuring in each case that it was clear who should implement them. Common themes in these recommendations were summarized to form the focus for critical discussions on the final morning of the seminar. The recommendations presented in Chapter 1 have grown out of these considerations, but the responsibility for them is now mine.

The Chapters in this Book
The seminar papers included in chapters in this book are to do with students and learning. One participant at the seminar thought it odd that a paper on continuing education in polytechnics and universities should be included in a seminar on the future of teaching in higher education. I apologize neither for its inclusion nor for its place as the leading paper.

It is not odd to start by thinking about changes in who is to be taught in higher education. Indeed the incessant debates on excellence or equality, the fall in the age participation rates, the number of qualified 18-year-olds and the postgraduate labour market are part of thinking about who higher education is for; and if, as is proposed here, older students will form a major proportion of the students in higher education in the future, all the issues discussed in the remaining chapters of this volume will be seen in a new light. Who our students are should strongly influence what we expect them to learn, how we expect them to learn it, and how we should teach and assess them.

The influence of who our students are draws attention to the overlapping and symbiotic relationship of continuing and higher education. The case for expanding opportunities in continuing education has always been based on the needs of older students, so it is here, and rightly so. What is often forgotten are the enormous potential benefits to the style of courses, of teaching and of learning in higher education if our polytechnics and universities were to adapt their teaching to a substantial proportion of older students.

Yet the benefits that older students might bring will only be obtained if the polytechnics and universities are sufficiently professional to be student-centred and sufficiently flexible to adapt their curricula. Yet professional flexibility must be neither fickle nor wayward. Chapter 3 attempts to set standards of professional flexibility.

To some readers Chapter 4 may seem out of place. Thinking chronologically they will expect it to appear after the chapter on teaching and learning. But that would be totally to miss the major themes of the chapter, namely, that assessment affects the achievement of curricular aims. Assessment affects the way students learn. Consequently, decisions on methods of assessment come after major decisions on the curriculum but before everyday decisions on how we should teach and learn.

Teaching and learning is not only a vast subject, it can be seen in so many different ways and contexts. It can be seen in the context of a systems analyst, of the objectives to be achieved, of the methods adopted, and of students' experiences. Professors Paul Black and John Sparkes have attempted the impossible task of accommodating all these viewpoints simultaneously, not only for completeness and because they each have their own value, but also because experience shows that recommendations on teaching and learning are often misunderstood by people who do not view them in the same context.

ACKNOWLEDGEMENTS

The consultative process that led to the recommendations in this monograph means that there are many people to be thanked for their contributions.

I am most grateful to Professor Gareth Williams for his support and advice on the procedure I have adopted, to Sir Bruce Williams for his quiet authoritative chairmanship, to all the authors whose ideas and written contributions were subjected to comment and criticism that was more than usually public in the early stages, to Miss Betty Hollinshead, Mr. Trevor Habeshaw, Dr Alex Main, Professor Peter Ayscough and Dr David Armstrong for organizing fruitful pre-seminars so willingly and efficiently and without any thought of reward, to Mrs Betsy Breuer for her accommodating organization, to Sally Kington for her professional approach to the publication, to the University of Exeter for allowing me to spend so much time on this work, and most of all, to Mrs. Lynne Griffiths who conquered the worst frustrations of mastering a word-processor and who has typed and re-typed not only many drafts of the chapters but many versions of the preliminary sheets, containing propositions, counter-propositions and their respective arguments, which contributed to the discussions from which the chapters eventually evolved.

Donald Bligh
Editor

SEMINAR PARTICIPANTS

Sir Bruce Williams (Chairman)
*Dr David Armstrong, University of London
*Professor Peter Ayscough, University of Leeds
Mr Ron Barnett, Council for National Academic Awards
Professor Tony Becher, University of Sussex
+ Professor Paul Black, Chelsea College, University of London
+ Dr Donald Bligh, University of Exeter (Convenor)
Mr John Davidson, Bristol Polytechnic
+ Professor Lewis Elton, University of Surrey
Mr Norman Evans, Policy Studies Institute
Mr Colin Flood Page
Mr Dennis Fox, Trent Polytechnic
+ Dr Sinclair Goodlad, Imperial College, University of London
+ Dr Richard Hoggart, Goldsmiths' College, University of London
Sir Norman Lindop, Hatfield Polytechnic
*Dr Alex Main, University of Strathclyde
Dr Alan Matterson, Kingston Polytechnic
Professor Emeritus Roy Niblett
Mr John O'Leary, *The Times Higher Education Supplement*
Mr Andrew Pearmain, National Union of Students
Mrs Pauline Perry, Department of Education and Science
+ Professor Sir Brian Pippard, University of Cambridge
Dr Anthony Pointon, Association of Polytechnic Teachers
Professor Alec Ross, University of Lancaster
Ms. Patricia Santinelli, *The Times Higher Education Supplement*
+ Mr Richard Smethurst, University of Oxford
+ Professor John Sparkes, The Open University
Dr Geoffrey Squires, University of Hull
+ Professor Michael Stephens, University of Nottingham
Professor Campbell Stewart, University of Sussex
Dr Graham Stodd, West Sussex Institute of Higher Education
+ Mr John Taylor, Advisory Council for Adult and Continuing Education
Dr William Taylor, University of London Institute of Education
Mr Malcolm Tight, Birkbeck College, University of London
Mrs Mary Warnock, Hertford College, University of Oxford
Mr David Warren Piper, University of London Institute of Education
Professor Gareth Williams, University of Lancaster

+ Author of paper   * Convenor of pre-seminar

1

RECOMMENDATIONS FOR LEARNING

by Donald Bligh

Teaching in higher education needs to be pursued with more professionalism and more flexibility. These were the two major conclusions of the seminar. My recommendations arising from the final discussions of the seminar are as follows.

THE NEED FOR MORE PROFESSIONALISM
1   *Professional Peer Review. Institutions of higher education should ensure that the design of courses and the processes of teaching, learning and assessment are more open than they are at present, and are subject to regular peer reviews.*
1.1   *Whilst recognizing that curricula in higher education must reflect the content, methods and inner logic of the disciplines being studied, teachers should ensure that they neglect neither practice nor theory, and that they take account of the needs both of society and of the individual.*
1.2   *Courses should be manifestly student-centred.*
1.2a   *Teachers in higher education should explain clearly to students the aims, structure, procedures, requirements and methods of assessment (if relevant) of their courses.*
1.2b   *Teachers should help students to take maximum responsibility for their own learning.*
1.2c   *Courses should be designed to focus upon the tasks through which students will acquire and display excellence both of mind and of practical skills rather than upon the exposition of a series of topics by teachers.*
1.2d   *Styles of teaching should be developed such that working relationships between teachers and students are valued by both.*
1.3   *Institutional reviews of their assessment procedures for students should examine*
   a   The relationship of assessments to curricular aims.
   b   The variety and reliability of assessment methods used.
   c   The methods of communicating results.
   d   The grading system adopted.
2   *Professional Improvement.*
2.1   *Institutions should encourage faculty boards and academic departments to appoint or designate staff to have special expertise in the study of the teaching and learning of their*

subjects. These specialists will, with their colleagues, work on the design and management of courses.

2.2 *Professional development units should concentrate upon the education and training of such specialists and, in collaboration with the specialists, upon the professional induction and development of new staff.*

THE NEED FOR MORE FLEXIBILITY

3 *Flexibility in Teaching. While maintaining academic standards, institutions and validating bodies should encourage more flexible patterns of, and access to, courses for individuals in higher education.*

3.1 *A feasibility study should inquire how far it is possible to assess experiential learning for entry to, or exemption from, specific courses.*

3.2 *A study should investigate the feasibility of providing more opportunities for students (on payment of fees) to be assessed for higher education qualifications without having taken a specific route to prepare for the assessment.*

3.3 *A working party should be set up to study the feasibility and desirability of new patterns of degree courses.*

3.4 *Institutions in higher education should be prepared to place much more emphasis upon the needs of older students.*

4 *Flexibility in Staffing. Institutions should take steps to maintain and increase*
   a   The mobility of staff by industrial, commercial and professional transfer, secondment and exchange.
   b   Study-leave.
   c   The use of part-time and temporary staff.

THE NEED FOR MORE PROFESSIONALISM

The demand for more professionalism is a demand to act in a professional manner; that is, to behave as members of professions behave.

But what are the distinguishing marks of professional behaviour? It seems to me that professional activity requires considerable skill, expecially judgement, in non-routine and possibly complex situations (cf. Hoyle 1980). The skill and judgement is achieved by applying an organized body of knowledge in the light of a code of professional values, or principles. The values are, or at least should be, derived from the needs of clients. Within the limits of these professional values, members of professions claim freedoms based upon their special knowledge: individuality in style of practice, and a considerable degree of autonomy from government or other interference. (See SRHE Leverhulme 7 (Bligh 1982) Chapter 4.)

Notice it is primarily their specialist knowledge which is used to justify their freedoms, their claims to serve the interests of their clients, and, commonly, the right to exclude others, who do not have the knowledge, from doing their job. This knowledge is normally acquired over a lengthy period of education or training, often in higher education. Notice too, that it is organized knowledge that is relevant. The possession of experience alone is not enough, unless the learning from that experience has been generalized and organized so that the relevant items of knowledge can be selected and then applied appropriately. Nor need the organized knowledge necessarily be highly theoretical, although it sometimes is.

Architects, lawyers, doctors and consultant engineers are all professionals in the sense I have outlined. They have spent several years in higher education acquiring an organized body of knowledge, some of which is theoretical and some of which is simply organized in a useful way. They also acquire their status and qualifications after some practical experience during their training, or on the job, or both. It is in their interests to serve the interests of their clients, because ultimately their reputation and their incomes depend upon client satisfaction.

How 'professional' are we as *teachers* in higher education in these respects? Certainly we claim considerable autonomy from government interference. We are allowed great individuality in our styles of teaching (cf Ch. 5:11). But although we have a code of practice, it is only partly based upon the needs of students, our clients. (Indirectly we have other clients.) Most of all, although we have had a long education and training in higher education, it was *not* a training for our role as teachers. It was for our role as chemists, physicists, geographers and so on.

We do not in general possess an organized body of knowledge about teaching but we could seek to acquire it. When most of us start to teach in higher education, we know little more about teaching than our clients. Our training, in many cases, is less than one week. Consequently, in practice, there is no reason to expect that we can exercise great skill or judgement in a complex and non-routine job like teaching. Indeed the lack of variety in, for example, modes of courses, techniques of teaching and methods of assessment shows how academic staff may have turned complex tasks into routine ones. (cf Ch. 2:3.7).

The routines become fixed when we do not systematically review what we do. With neither systematic reviews nor an extensive training, it is difficult to appreciate the sublety of the teaching tasks on which we are engaged. In both these respects we could be more professional.

Hence the demand for more professionalism has two aspects.

1 As teachers we constantly need to review what we are doing in order to improve it.
2 We need to develop ways to accomplish the improvements.

However, before we turn to recommendations to further these two aspects it is necessary to make a digression. Professionalism is more than knowledge: it involves a frame of mind which cannot easily be described but is assumed both in this volume and the next. A teacher is not only a geographer, physicist, engineer or whatever; he is essentially a teacher. Clearly a frame of mind is not something a few pages can supply. I can only hint at it.

For many academic staff the starting point in planning their teaching is their academic subject. Decisions about the content of courses — what is to be taught — are uppermost in their minds. For some 'what is to be taught' consists of information to be learned. Others pay more attention to the skills, in particular the patterns of thought, that students must acquire.

It is a further step to be able to analyse one's discipline in terms of its skills, because to do so requires re-conceiving separate topics within one's subject in terms of their associated patterns of thought, rather than in terms of their subject matter. Amongst such patterns of thought are the ability to doubt, to distinguish, to think of ways to test the truth of what one is told, to find words to say what one does not understand, to ask 'what would I have done in the circumstances?', to tolerate the uncertainty of ignorance and knowledge, to argue another person's point of view, to appreciate how another person may feel, to be able to 'crack open' a problem, to look for connections and analogies between different parts of a discipline, to think of instances of a generalization, to make a value judgement after bringing together a mass of evidence, and to ask 'what would count as an answer to a question?' and 'what kind of evidence could there be to answer it?' Clearly it would be possible to make this list a very long one. I have confined it to items that may be relevant in more than one subject. Each of these patterns of thought is different and requires different teaching techniques.

It is yet another step to be able to see the whole of one's subject in terms of a series of skills building upon each other, because to design a course for students so that each skill — each pattern of thought — builds upon earlier ones, requires taking one's subject to bits and reconstructing it according to how its patterns of thought can best be learned. The structure for learning a subject may be quite different from either its logical structure or the way its knowledge is classified. In biology for example, knowledge is classified into groups and sub-groups of animals and plants, culminating in their genera and species. To classify knowledge in this way is not to present a living subject or to show the logic of how it fits together (ie its unity as a discipline). On the contrary, the classification concentrates on ever finer divisions.

There may be more than one logical structure of a subject. One logic of biology, evolution, starts with some general principles (some of which can be quite abstract, if you consider the genetics of how species come to vary) and then traces the adaptations and transformations of species through time, with reference to many different classes, orders, families, genera and species.

However, neither the classification of plants and animals nor the logic of evolution, provides a suitable structure for a course. A course based only on a classification of plants and animals would be utterly tedious, while a course based on the history of evolution may present some of its most difficult concepts to the newest and least able students.

What is required is a course that elicits the sheer fascination of understanding plants and animals (eg 'How on earth do centipedes co-ordinate all those legs with so little brain?') and then progressively uses that curiosity to lead the student to techniques of observation, to the capacity to ask questions, to hypothesize answers, to test the answers, and to criticize them. But as soon as we talk in these terms we are talking about students' motivation (eg their curiosity), their powers of perception (eg techniques of observation), their powers of reasoning (eg testing ideas), and so on. In other words we are talking about devising a course to match the mental needs and abilities of the students. It is much more than mastery of one's subject. Mastery of one's subject is essential, but not enough for a professional approach to teaching.

Yet in a way, the contrast I have made is a false one; for to be able to take one's subject to bits and to re-structure it in many different ways, devising all manner of different problems to cultivate patterns of thought, is, indeed, to have mastery of one's subject. It shows mastery on many different planes.

The point is that to be a professional teacher involves the ability to restructure one's subject using the student's construction of concepts. To do so is one essential ingredient of being student-centred as well as (not 'rather than') subject-centred. That is why this book is *Professionalism and Flexibility for Learning*, not *Professionalism and Flexibility in Teaching*.

However, that is not all a professional teacher needs to know. He does not need to know all the research literature on students, teaching, learning, assessment and so on; but he needs to know that it exists, where to find it, how to use it, and to have an attitude which recognizes that it is relevant. In the same way that a doctor spends years acquiring a background in anatomy, physiology, biochemistry and so on, and then applies his knowledge in a multitude of techniques for discerning the needs of his patients, for treating them, and for evaluating the effects of the treatment he gives them, so a teacher needs some background knowledge to use a wide variety of techniques, to understand his students, to help them, to assess their progress, and to evaluate his own performance.

These techniques are essential to the craft of a professional teacher but the art of teaching is more than its craft. A teacher's art lies in adapting and combining his techniques in creative ways. Creativity is a mark of good teaching. In this sense teaching is an art requiring both knowledge and skill. Like other arts it develops by informed appreciation and criticism. For this reason it needs to be more open. Only then can improvements be developed.

Recommendation 1. Professional Peer Review
Institutions of higher education should ensure that the design of courses and the processes of teaching, learning and assessment are more open than they are at present, and are subject to regular peer reviews.

As in Popper's 'open' society (1958), these activities will be 'open' when they are subject to the processes of free critical inquiry that are the basis of higher education itself.

By saying that these activities should be more 'open' I mean they should be more freely observed, informatively appreciated and rationally discussed, by staff and by students. (cf Ch.5:7a and 10). What is needed are more teachers with an attitude of mind in which they no longer feel their authority and esteem are threatened by constructive comment. Rather we should seek an atmosphere in which all teachers and students help each other in trying to learn. It is a process of working together openly, honestly, without presenting a front and without fear of humiliation.

It is in this sense that teaching and learning are too often regarded as private and not 'open'. Few teachers invite others to observe and discuss their techniques of teaching. Few students discuss their techniques of studying. The language of teaching and learning is not greatly used, or indeed known, by those engaged in it. Language provides the framework and the tools — the concepts for understanding. Without them understanding is limited. Language also enhances self-awareness; and an understanding of oneself is essential for good teaching. The restricted use of the language of teaching and learning suggests that teachers and students alike could have a greater understanding of what they are doing (see for example Ch. 4, Ch.5:1, 4a, 7, 9, 12, and Ch. 2:1 in SRHE Leverhulme 7).

Increased openness requires more confidence and hence much more mutual support. Openness can encourage more teamwork amongst staff. In the public sector teamwork is becoming more common in course planning, but the convention that only one teacher at a time should meet a class of students is extraordinary. To observe an open intellectual responsiveness of experts in a discipline is an experience of higher education too rarely available to most students.

Openness should extend to those in similar disciplines in other institutions (cf. Ch. 2:3.3). *Particularly in vocational subjects or fields, curricula should be developed after discussions with professional associations and other relevant organizations.* (By 'curricula' I mean not only the subject matter of a course, but everything to do with its design, including the methods of teaching, learning and assessment.) To recommend the greater involvement of professional associations is not to say that they should have control of curricula. Indeed the seminar was concerned that their influence is sometimes excessive and occasionally ill-informed. Nevertheless, it was felt that in most areas of study the role of outside practitioners could usefully be extended rather than reduced.

Openness is necessary for effective peer reviews. Peer review is a process of professional observation, discussion and judgement. It may be formal or informal. Peer reviews have several direct uses: (i) they may be used formally to improve 'teaching' in the widest meaning of that word; (ii) they provide necessary information to guide individual members of staff in their career development, the development of their teaching skills, and in other personal ways (see Ch. 2:5.4 and 5.5 in SRHE Leverhulme 7); (iii) they may be used for promotion purposes; (iv) external examiners also have a review role; (v) peer reviews may be used to validate courses as indeed they are by the CNAA and other organizations; (vi) they might also be used, as the UGC may appear to do, to inform decisions on the allocation of resources.

The purposes are different and it would be unwise to use reviews designed for one purpose to achieve the purposes of another. The criteria may overlap, but they will not be the same. The first three attend to different professional needs of an individual; the last three are more concerned with the evaluation of courses, departments and institutions.

Regular peer reviews also bring indirect benefits to teaching. They provide incentives for staff. By establishing educational values and standards, they help to weed out bad practices. They encourage innovations and developments in teaching by making staff think carefully about what they are doing. They raise the visible status of teaching. They give staff the opportunity to demonstrate to others their excellence as teachers. They provide occasions when knowledge and ideas about teaching are disseminated; and they bring together senior staff in related disciplines to exercise judgement in matters of teaching.

Peer reviews are essentially confined to teachers (cf Ch. 5:6 and 7a). They are *by* teachers *of* teachers. They are not evaluations by students, representatives of other professional bodies, or inspectors, although these groups may have a role at the discretion of the teachers involved. Peer reviews should be professional in the sense that they are judgements requiring special skills based upon a body of specialist knowledge and practical experience; they entail a code of practice or ethics. They are occasions when professions exercise their autonomy, not least with reference to who they admit to their own membership.

In the context of higher education, peer reviews are also professional activities in the sense that they employ values which the profession would wish to characterize all its activities — the search for truth, the use of observation and rational judgement, and the striving for high quality in all we do. These are the values which should drive higher education itself (Ch. 5:7b).

One idea canvassed at the seminar was that *There should be an ombudsman whose judgement may be sought on the quality of teaching.* I am sympathetic towards this idea. It involves two principles: the first is the principle of consulting external referees, which is well established in the evaluation of research. Secondly, there is the principle of appeal to an independent agency outside the immediate circle of personal relationships. It is to be expected that many heads of departments and others who should be responsible for cultivating an open climate and organizing internal peer reviews will claim that they already carry out peer reviews to improve teaching, to give career advice, to assess candidates for promotion, and so on. No doubt some of these purposes are pursued in some institutions; but that is to miss the point of formalizing peer reviews: *new standards of professional competence need to be established, and this includes competence in peer reviews too.* We need to develop accepted standards and procedures in the evaluation of teaching as we have in the evaluation of research.

New standards require new criteria. Clearly it is not possible to state them all here, or all the practices that might be observed and discussed, before making a judgement. Chapters on the curriculum (Ch.3), on assessment for learning (Ch.4) and on teaching and learning (Ch.5), particularly Chapter 5, give some criteria.

The following criteria for peer reviews are presented as a sample of the ideas suggested during the seminar. No group of recommendations, if implemented, could improve teaching to complete perfection. The effects will be cumulative and interactive.

Recommendation 1.1 *Whilst recognizing that curricula in higher education must reflect the content, methods and inner logic of the disciplines being studied, teachers should ensure that they neglect neither practice nor theory, and that they take account of the needs both of society and of the individual.*

This is not to say that every element of every course should contain all these components (theory, practice, society and the individual), but there are dangers if one is neglected by over-concentration on another (see figure on page 73). A course that concentrates excessively on the practical applications of a discipline risks leaving too little time for students to study the subject in depth, to develop an intellectual curiosity about a subject, to recognize the beauty of its generalizations, or to appreciate its intrinsic value; while a course that concentrates too much upon theory may produce students who cannot see the relevance of their subject to the complexity of the modern world, who cannot relate it to their inner life, and who perceive higher education as irrelevant to their later life. Courses that concentrate excessively upon the needs of society risk moving in a direction that exploits the individual to serve the state, that assaults intellectual freedom, and that ignores some of the understandable feelings of students such as their need to search for self-identity (Ch. 2:3.6). On the other hand courses that over-concentrate on the needs of individuals may result in self-indulgent students, an unwieldy variety of curricula, an overall lack of intellectual synthesis or coherence, and a poor appreciation of the social context of academic work.

Recommendation 1.2   Courses should be manifestly student-centred.

That is to say that teachers should be able to demonstrate to their peers, and to their students, that their courses are adapted to the needs of their consumers, the students. I do not mean that courses should be adapted so that everything is within a student's grasp. Sometimes it is right to lead students to the edge of the unknown and to what cannot yet be understood. It is a matter of mutual support in the struggle to understand one's subject and to discipline oneself. I have argued that client-centredness is a mark of professions and professionalism. Student-centredness is an attitude of mind. There is no final check list of student-centredness that can be used in peer reviews, but members of the seminar thought the following practices important.

Recommendation 1.2a   Teachers in higher education should explain clearly to students the aims, structure, procedures, requirements and methods of assessment (if relevant) of their courses.

By 'structure' I particularly mean the ways in which the content and methods of the course are organized so that they develop. 'Requirements' are more concerned with what the students are expected to do during the course than with what they were expected to have done before entering.

It is not enough to give clear and explicit statements of these things; they must be explained and open to criticism from students and staff alike (Ch. 5:1—5 especially 3). That is not to say that teachers should be obliged to act upon students' criticisms. Explanation and criticism are intrinsic not only as ends but as means to higher education. Consequently, explanations about a course are not a preliminary to that course, but part of it, because they enhance a student's understanding of his subject. Explanations also ensure that staff know what each other is doing, which improves team work.

One reason for this recommendation, but not the only one, is that without such explanations students cannot maximize their responsibility for their own learning (Ch. 5:5). Hence this recommendation is closely associated with a second.

Recommendation 1.2b   Teachers should help students to take maximum responsibility for their own learning.

To assert the responsibility of students is not to say that teachers in higher education can now renounce their responsibility for students' learning — far from it. Teachers set academic standards and encourage the patterns of thought that constitute their discipline (Ch. 3:1.1—2.3, 4.1 and 13; Ch. 5:8). But it does imply that teachers should devise courses in such a way that students can plan how they are going to work and how they are going to discipline themselves (Ch. 5:4 and 5). It does not necessarily mean that students should spend longer working independently in private study. They may plan to work with their fellow students with periods of writing, in formal discussion and helping each other. Nor does it mean that contact between staff and students would be reduced; quite the contrary. For example, by devising courses focused upon a series of tasks, rather than upon a series of lectures, staff may spend longer working *with* students informally.

This example draws attention to two further features of student-centred courses.

Recommendation 1.2c   Courses should be designed to focus upon the tasks through which students will acquire and display excellence both of mind and of practical skills, rather than upon the exposition of a series of topics by teachers.

This is not just an invocation to academic staff to think of their students rather than themselves, important as that may be (Ch.3:1.3). It is a plea to raise academic standards by placing less emphasis upon the acquisition of information from lectures, books and other presentations (Ch.3:2.1 and 4.1; Ch.5:4a). It is a recommendation that peer reviews of teaching should concentrate upon students' activities because it is particularly through activities that students learn. It is a plea to make students work upon projects requiring high level mental and practical skills, particularly those employed in solving problems, and from which students may obtain feedback on their own learning and an opportunity to diagnose their own weaknesses (Ch.2:3.6, Ch.3:3.4, Ch.5:2 and 4c). Task-centred courses also provide an opportunity for creativity, personal sensitivity and the development of the arts of visual and spoken communication.

Recommendation 1.2d   Styles of teaching should be developed such that working relationships between teachers and students are valued by both.

As Black and Sparkes portray vividly (Ch.5:1), the informal, helping relationship is the one most valued by students. Whatever the administrative fictions about contact hours, lectures are not, in most cases, periods for a meeting of minds. They are not, in practice, periods of interaction between teacher and student (Ch.5:4).

The emphasis on relationships is not a criticism of distance learning. Institutions such as the Open University have worked hard through their media to develop working relationships, albeit not very personal ones;

and to compensate for this tenuous personal contact they have student groups, counsellors, summer schools and so on, as well as a highly student-centred approach in other respects (see for example, Recommendations 1.2a—c).

Other institutions should take advantage of their relatively favourable staff-student ratios to develop excellent working relationships between staff and students.

Recommendation 1.3   Institutional reviews of their assessment procedures for students should examine

a   The relationship of assessment to curricular aims.
b   The variety and reliability of assessment methods used.
c   The methods of communicating results.
d   The grading system adopted.

These points are made in the chapter on assessment for learning (Ch.4) and the reader is referred to them.

The purpose of this recommendation is to create procedures by which academic staff, who appreciate the variety and subtlety of their own curricular aims, might also agree upon the implications of these aims for assessment. As soon as the wide diversity of forms of thought in any discipline is appreciated, it will be recognized that a diversity of methods of assessment is required. This is not to say that a different method of assessment is required for every form of thought examined. It is rather that the crudity of many assessment methods and the ways in which we commonly display the results, do justice neither to the students, nor to the furtherance of their disciplines. The process of assessment could be a process of discrimination both between one student and another and between the different levels of attainment by an individual on a wide variety of skills. Yet the weakness of assessment instruments, and the techniques with which they are used, lies in their lack of discrimination.

Recommendation 2. Professional Improvement

Recommendation 2.1   Institutions should encourage faculty boards and academic departments to appoint or designate staff to have special expertise in the study of the teaching and learning of their subjects. These specialists will, with their colleagues, work on the design and management of courses.

Recommendation 2.2   Professional development units should concentrate upon the education and training of such specialists and, in collaboration with the specialists, upon the professional induction and development of new staff.

Professional development is a necessary concomitant of course review and institutions should explicitly recognize and exercise their responsibility for it. It would be unreasonable for staff reviews and outside bodies to criticize courses without there being any provision for subsequent improvement. A similar, though not the same, principle is assumed in the Employment Acts, which require training as a necessary concomitant of probationary periods of employment — 'Don't stand there and criticize. Help me do something about it.'

The fundamental difficulty in implementing improvements in response to peer reviews is that some improvements require not only a detailed knowledge of the theories, concepts and inner logic of the specialist subject, but also a knowledge of the principles of course design, research into teaching, learning and assessment methods, or whatever is the area of improvement required. These two sets of knowledge are rarely found in the same person.

What is required is substantial co-operation between educational and subject specialists. With the small number of educational specialists in most institutions, there is no way in which they could relate to all staff, particularly bearing in mind the difficulties outlined in the paper on professional development (see Ch.2:3 and 4 in SRHE Leverhulme Volume 7).

One way over this difficulty might be for the educational specialist to pass on his knowledge in depth to a limited number of subject specialists. For educational specialists to attempt to spread their knowledge more thinly would result in a little learning being a dangerous thing. For example, while it is clearly desirable for teachers to be able to say what they want their students to achieve before the students are asked to achieve it, a superficial understanding of the use of objectives in education has led the whole idea of using them into disrepute.

It is difficult to say exactly how subject specialists should work. This will depend upon the department and its personalities.

However there are three difficulties in this proposal. Firstly it is doubtful how successfully the knowledge would be passed on. The members of staff designated in departments would not acquire the educational knowledge to the same depth as those from whom they had learned unless they took their task very seriously indeed for a long time, or there were an incentive (a qualification or increment?) and some check on their learning.

Secondly, in many departments such individuals would be under strong social pressure from their departmental colleagues not to pursue their new role. In universities the AUT/UAP Agreement made provision ten years ago for a senior departmental colleague to pursue a continuing role to assist new staff after initial induction and training courses. This provision has been largely ignored.

Thirdly, if a departmental nominee can only acquire his special knowledge, skills and values of teaching after a lengthy period of training, there is a danger that too many teachers in higher education will leave the departmental nominee to worry about improving teaching, while they get on with other things. In this case the recommendation would lead to a declining interest in teaching amongst the very people whose interest should be increased.

Within the limits of resources, the obvious policy is to raise the standard of initial training so that, in time, every teacher will have some systematic knowledge of basic principles and research which should inform course design, teaching, learning, assessment and the evaluation of the teacher's own performance. Years of experience on the job do not teach these fundamentals.

THE NEED FOR MORE FLEXIBILITY
Like the demand for more professionalism, the demand for more flexibility has two aspects: one concerned with the varied provision of courses and wider opportunities for teaching, learning and assessment; and the other concerned with provisions for staff. The recommendations overlap; but that is a strength, not a weakness.

Recommendation 3. Flexibility in Teaching
While maintaining academic standards, institutions and validating bodies should encourage more flexible patterns of, and access to, courses for individuals in higher education.

Flexibility implies a willingness to change; and change will lead to diversity. Diversity should be encouraged. While it would not be wise to abolish, or drastically diminish, the full-time single Honours three- or four-year degree courses for recent school leavers, this one kind of course dominates the provision in nearly all subject areas. The lack of provision for other courses cannot, in the long run, be good for students, employers or higher education itself.

Obviously there are administrative and academic difficulties, but institutions should make greater efforts to allow students to leave and return, to change courses, to transfer to other institutions of higher education, and to blend courses across faculties and across institutions (Ch.2:4.1). While there are some advantages in uninterrupted study, it is not obvious that intercalated periods of practical work are so harmful to the study of science, engineering and professional subjects that institutional regulations should manifestly inhibit the contribution of wider experience to academic study (Ch.3:2.2). Sandwich courses are not obviously disastrous. Language tutors speak highly of the development of their students during a year abroad; so it is not obvious that the maturity required in the study of other humanities is so in flower at the age of eighteen that only full-time non-stop courses are worth while.

Institutions should also allow more varied patterns of participation, particularly for part-time students, at all levels, Employers need more diversity of associated skills which could be provided if more varied paths through the educational system were possible. At present, for example, it is not anticipated that a geographer interested in river flows should attend classes on fluid mechanics in engineering. The effect upon the student is discouragement. With the development of credit transfer facilities, there could be many more viable non-degree courses. Many of them could be partly composed of elements from existing courses. Institutions of higher education should become more of a diverse national resource and less like private clubs, with membership rules and codes of behaviour.

Before making specific recommendations for greater flexibility, their feasibility and likely consequences usually need to be researched. For example, Toyne (1979) has carried out such research in the area of credit transfer. Clearly there are limits to possible flexibility resulting from limited resources and the nature of some disciplines, but while there may have been good reasons for discouraging diversity in the past, it is necessary to find out whether those reasons still carry weight. For example, if there is now a contraction of student numbers, in some institutions there may now be less pressure on accommodation than before.

For these reasons feasibility studies are recommended (Ch.2:3.6, 3.8, 3.9 and 3.11). In particular three areas need further study.

Recommendation 3.1   A feasibility study should inquire how far it is possible to assess experiential learning for entry to, or exemption from, specific courses.

By 'experiential learning' I mean the knowledge and skills derived from working and other experiences in life.

Clearly, students enter courses with very varied backgrounds so that to judge whether mature students' experience qualifies them to enter a course at the beginning is very different from judging whether their previous experience exempts them from covering the ground of, say, a first-year course. The latter requires assessment of a particular knowledge rather than a general ability or general background. Nonetheless, in both cases the assessment of knowledge and skills derived from experience should be confined to that which is relevant to the courses to be undertaken. For example, what are the relevant qualities that motherhood bestows? Mothers are usually dependable and willing to accept modestly paid employment; but what credit, for example, should be given for dependability? Does higher education give credit for qualities that an employer would later find valuable when combined with academic qualifications? While the Policy Studies Institute has begun to study this field, the answers to these and many other questions are needed before many institutions will make their regulations more flexible with comfort (cf. Ch.2:3.8, 3.9, 3.11 and 4.1).

Recommendation 3.2 A study should investigate the feasibility of providing more opportunities for students (on payment of fees) to be assessed for higher education qualifications without having taken a specific route to prepare for the assessment.

There is nothing new in the principle behind this proposal. Examinations have long been available from the Associated Board of the Royal Schools of Music without any process of selection and tuition by that college. It is doubtful whether this has reduced the amount or quality of musical performance amongst the population as a whole, and it may have encouraged and improved it. This proposal assumes that the study for qualifications in higher education is something generally to be encouraged rather than something restricted to people resident in particular institutions. With encouragement to increase the number of home-based students, presumably residence on campus is no longer regarded as essential for many qualifications.

London University has for a long time offered an 'External Degree' qualification to candidates who pursue courses by any number of routes independently of the London colleges. Admittedly the University of London has recently considered closing this facility, but there is no reason in principle why it should not be extended to other institutions.

There are some subjects where such a provision would be impossible because unexaminable practical experience forms an essential part of the course. It may also be thought that the Open University largely satisfies the remaining need, but not everyone seeking qualifications or an education may wish or need to work under the course work pressures of the Open University, or seek the courses the Open University provides.

This recommendation must be seen within the wider call for flexibility. It is in no way confined to degree courses. Indeed it may be particularly appropriate for short courses. It may also be suitable for students who, for one reason or another, dropped out of full-time higher education and wish to complete their course of studies part-time, thereby making use of the investment that has been placed in them (Ch.2:4.3). (Fewer than half the students who drop out of universities do so because they fail an examination.)

The proposal to be considered here should favour part-time students and, as Malcolm Tight (1982) has shown, there is still a great need for part-time higher education (Ch.2:2.5).

Recommendation 3.3 A working party should be set up to study the feasibility and desirability of new patterns of degree courses.

I have to confess to some apprehension in making this recommendation. It is clear that there needs to be some way of making patterns of courses more flexible. Three-year Honours degrees are not ordained by God as the optimum pattern unto eternity. But responsibility for courses is so diffused that it is not obvious by whom such a working party should be set up, or that anyone will take any notice of its pronouncements. There is no organization for higher education equivalent to the Schools Council.

Proposition 3.3 in the chapter on the curriculum (Ch.3) is for what has become known as the 2 + 2 system. Participants at the seminar saw many weaknesses in this specific proposal. It would require an enormous adjustment by staff in both schools and higher education. There were fears that academic standards would be lowered by reducing the length of degree courses. Although there have been precedents for short degree courses in Britain before the Second World War, in the Commonwealth and in Scotland, Britain already has shorter undergraduate courses than most European countries. Participants saw wide differences between the demands of different disciplines. In some disciplines students seem to be 'burnt out' by their third year; in others, it was claimed, there is a necessary two-year groundwork before the meat of the course can be digested in the third year. The idea that only the best students should proceed to the second two years was regarded as élitist by some participants (although that is already the case with postgraduate courses). Furthermore, the 2 + 2 system cannot easily run alongside a three-year system. The two-year DipHE has not attracted many students, but this could be because three-year degree courses with three-year grants have been available, and to obtain a degree after the DipHE requires a further two years in some colleges.

Despite these powerful objections, the question remains, 'Why should a three- or four-year course be considered the optimal pattern for courses for all subjects?' Part of the answer lies in assumptions to do with the comparability of degrees and the competition for jobs between graduating students. But as soon as we get away from the idea that higher education is something we complete at the age of twenty-one, never to return, these assumptions will be weakened.

A system of entitlement to two years' grant in the first instance followed by a further two-year grant, could go some way to changing the pattern of demand as well as being economically attractive (cf Ch.2:3.10). Would such a financial constraint upon the length of courses be an infringement of academic freedom? I do not think it would, but that is an issue to be taken up in *Accountability or Freedom for Teachers*? (SRHE Leverhulme 7).

The 2 + 2 system is only one of many possible patterns. Short courses have the advantage of increasing the flexibility and diversity of educational experience. An alternative would be to make secondary education cease at sixteen, to be followed by three years in a sixth form or further education college, so that a two-year Bachelors degree would start a year later than at present; or rather, it would start at a higher standard equivalent to one more year's work. A postgraduate Masters

RECOMMENDATIONS FOR LEARNING 27

degree would then take a further two years.

This arrangement has a number of attractions. In so far as such a proposal would use the natural tendency for 'academic drift' (Ch.2:2.3), it would probably be more acceptable amongst teachers. It would reduce divisiveness between academic and vocational courses in the further education sector if individuals took a mixture of these courses. If, as is possible, this arrangement increased educational participation in the 16—19 age range, some aspects of unemployment could be eased. Staff from contracting colleges of education might be able to redeploy their knowledge and skills to what is now first-year undergraduate level. The costs of undergraduate higher education would be reduced. The length of Masters courses would be increased from nine to twenty-one months and their standard would be correspondingly raised without any overall increase in the number of students in the higher education sector.

Clearly there could be many patterns of courses, less radical than either of these two, which could introduce flexibility into the higher education system. They too should be investigated.

Recommendation 3.4   Institutions in higher education should be prepared to place much more emphasis upon the needs of older students.

By 'older students' I particularly mean those who have returned to education having had a break after their initial period of education (Ch.2:2.1).

The decline in the 18-year-old population, the rapidity of technological development, the increasing need for career change, the increasing leisure associated with changing life styles and the need for retraining after a period of high unemployment, all point to a higher proportion of adult students in higher education (Ch.2:1). These issues are argued in Chapter 2.

What is needed is a general change in attitudes towards the education of adults (Ch.2:2.7 and 3.7) rather than a specific policy or decision. Consequently this recommendation is not directed for action at any one level of administration, at any particular type of institution, or at individuals with any special responsibilities. It is directed at everybody involved in higher education.

It is a recommendation to bear the needs of adults in mind whenever decisions are taken. When forming criteria for admission to higher education we must remember to ask what account has been taken of the needs of older students whose circumstances may have prevented them from competing for entry on equal terms with the majority of applicants (see Recommendation 8 in Fulton 1981) (cf also Ch.2:3.8, 3.9, and 4.1). When choosing the content of curricula we should take steps to allow the experience of adults to be relevantly used. When preparing the timetable we should not assume that all our students are aged eighteen and without family responsibilities. Adults have to be taught differently from students who have recently experienced the norms of school life. When choosing teaching methods we should actively seek ways to use the experience of adult students and this means actively reconsidering, and possibly changing our teaching methods every time we teach a topic. The ability to manage older students should, as a matter of course, be considered in the selection and training of teachers in higher education. Most examiners give credit for the relevant use of personal experience, but when designing assessments we should also consider what opportunities should be given to adult students to use the experiential learning not available to younger students.

These considerations are consistent with the proposal for a student-centred approach to teaching. For they imply that teachers must find out about the previous experience of their students. Flexibility in adapting our teaching to the background of the students is more rewarding than lecturing to a mass of unknown students and assuming them to be sieved into homogeneity by 'A' levels and without any experience which can enrich the learning of others.

Recommendation 4. Flexibility in Staffing

Institutions should take steps to maintain and increase

a   The mobility of staff by industrial, commercial and professional transfer, secondment and exchange.
b   Study-leave.
c   The use of part-time and temporary staff.

Stagnation is the major problem facing the staffing of higher education in the period up to the mid-1990s and possibly beyond. The chapter by Lindop and others in *Accountability or Freedom for Teachers*? (SRHE Leverhulme 7) shows that both in universities and polytechnics there is a preponderance of staff in the 35—45 age group (Bligh 1982). With the use of early retirement policies in response to the succession of cuts which higher education has recently suffered, the system faces a lengthy period when the rate of recruitment of new staff will be exceptionally low. Consequently, the constant re-invigoration so essential to creative endeavour will be lacking. The quality and quantity of research is bound to suffer. It will be seen by staff that few promotions are possible and this lack of incentives is likely to lead to despondency and frustration. There will also be a widening age gap between teachers and their students during a period that may see rapid social and technological change.

One way to ease this complex of difficulties must lie in increasing the diversity of experience available to staff in higher education. Increased participation by adult students will bring some diversity; but if students are to possess wider experience so must the staff. The best way to broaden the experience of relatively unchanging personnel, while maintaining the teaching function, is to increase short-term mobility. This can be done by organizing exchanges of staff between higher education, industry, the civil service, the professions and other areas of employment.

In the long run it is not in the interests of higher education to confine the use of study leave to narrow academic pursuits. No doubt higher education will continue to reward highly specialized research, but in teaching there will be a growing need for versatility; and versatility requires breadth. Breadth, too, must be rewarded where it serves the interests of good teaching.

The role of the practitioner in teaching music, medicine, art, architecture, law, accountancy and so on has long been recognized. The recognition should be extended to other disciplines. While this recommendation in no way implies that full-time staff should be made redundant to make way for part-time or temporary staff, the enrichment of teaching staff with recent practical experience should be maintained and, where possible, increased. Not only is it a matter for regret that in the present financial crisis part-time staff have been the first to be removed, it is unfortunate that in many institutions they do not have a place on senate and faculty boards where their practical experience could contribute to the design of curricula. In many fields it is important that professional experience should be fed into institutional decision making.

CONCLUSION

The recommendations of the SRHE Levehulme seminar on the teaching function go some way towards establishing professionalism and flexibility as broad principles. Recommendations 1 and 3 apply these principles to course design, teaching, learning, the assessment of students and the evaluation of teaching. Recommendations 2 and 4 direct these principles towards the needs of academic staff.

Underlying these recommendations is a need for new attitudes towards students, particularly older students; and it is towards the needs of older students we must now turn.

REFERENCES

Bligh, D.A. (Editor) (1982) *Accountability or Freedom for Teachers?* SRHE Leverhulme 7. Guildford: Society for Research into Higher Education

Hoyle, E. and Megarry, J. (Editors) (1980) *Professionalization and Deprofessionalization in Education. Professional Development of Teachers. World Yearbook of Education 1980* London: Kogan Page; New York: Nichols Publishing Co.

Popper, K.R. (1958) *The Open Society and its Enemies* Volume I. London: Routledge and Kegan Paul

Tight, M. (1982) *Part-time Degree Level Study in the United Kingdom* Leicester: ACACE

Toyne, P. (1979) *Education Credit Transfer: Feasibility Study* Final Report . Exeter

2

CONTINUING EDUCATION WITHIN UNIVERSITIES AND POLYTECHNICS

by Richard Hoggart, Michael Stephens, John Taylor and Richard Smethurst

INTRODUCTION

Continuing education is a vast field and this paper focuses on one aspect of it only: the relationship of the institutions of higher education, notably the universities and polytechnics, to adults other than their students of between 18—21 years old or thereabouts.

In this matter university attitudes have habitually varied. Some institutions, some university teachers, have welcomed the adult and the part-time student. It was the universities which in the nineteenth century created extra-mural education and, later, made common cause with the Workers' Education Association. Others in the universities are made uneasy by mature students. Do they have the right background and qualifications? Are they particularly demanding? Will they mix?

The polytechnics by their nature are more open to part-time and older students. Their main risk, which most but not all resist effectively, is of lapsing into 'academic drift'.

The current financial crisis within higher education and the certain prospect of a fall in the numbers of 18-year-olds is producing paradoxical effects. On the one hand, there is a greater readiness to accept part-time students. On the other is a tendency to withdraw even further behind the walls, concentrating on research and on the very highest level of young undergraduate (measured by 'A' level results).

One purpose of this paper is to argue that these two aims, each suitably qualified, need not be conflicting.

We do not underestimate the difficulties in the changes we propose. The rewards can be just as great — for the institutions themselves as their atmospheres change in response to the demands made and opportunities offered by a wider age range in their students and wider experiences than those of the 18-year-old; for students of all ages; and for specialists as they meet questioning of a sort that not all of them are at present subjected to. The mature student himself or herself is not, in short, the only beneficiary of the process we urge.

Our argument and the changes we propose are stated under the following propositions.

1.1 An adequate approach to continuing education requires a shift in focus from the institution to the student.

1.2 An educational system adequate to the needs of continuing education will be, above all, open to student needs. The student will have adequate purchasing power and adequate guidance.

1.3 The higher education system has provided some continuing education for more than a century; but opportunities for development have been missed. The main obstacle is in attitudes.

1.4 There are large disparities in the resources allocated to full-time and part-time students and, in the part-time sector, between vocational and non-vocational study.

1.5 Rapid technological development both demands regular updating and creates more leisure. These are the two 'main' grounds for transferring resources to continuing or post-initial education.

1.6 The use of continuing education to remedy earlier educational disadvantages is less acknowledged than its use in providing advanced further training.

2.1 Continuing education caters for all adults undertaking formal or non-formal study, full- or part-time, at any level and at any time after the completion of, and after a break from, their initial education at, and immediately following, school.

2.2 Staff attitudes are too much dominated by the 'front-end model' of education.

2.3 Historically, academic drift has often led to (i) a reduction in the provision and status of part-time and preparatory lower-level work; (ii) excessive concentration on 18-plus full-time students.

2.4 Expansion in the 1960s was a missed opportunity.

2.5 There is every reason to suppose that there is a substantial latent demand.

2.6 Part-time study is a main key to new developments in higher education.

3.1 The type of higher education normally available during the day should also be provided during evenings and weekends.

3.2 Every community with reasonable access to an institution of higher education should have its own centre suitably equipped for use by adult students. Such provision will have both professional and academic implications for staff.

3.3 There is a need for greater co-operation between educational and other institutions in the provision of continuing education.

3.4 Contracts for new academic staff should be broadly based and include a formal commitment to continuing education.

3.5 The professional development of teachers should include training for work with students in continuing education.

3.6 Curricula should be more flexible, so as to suit adult needs.

3.7 Teachers must be receptive to new teaching methods.

3.8 A great range of acceptable selection criteria, such as experiential credits, should be explored.

3.9 Wider acceptance of modular courses and credit transfer is

needed.
3.10 There should be financial provision for a universal entitlement to continuing education.
3.11 Research is needed on which to base changes in continuing education.
4.1 Recent initiatives reinforce the case for wider and more flexible access.
4.2 Recent developments give evidence of the need for local information and advisory services.
4.3 There have been some, but only a few studies of who adult students are.
4.4 Problems of financial support for adult students are still insufficiently considered.
4.5 Overall trends suggest there is growing recognition of the case for expanding continuing education.

WHY EMPHASIZE EDUCATION FOR ADULTS?

Definitions, Characteristics and Implications
The adaptation of further and higher education to suit the needs of adults has been variously called 'recurrent education', 'education permanente', 'lifelong learning', 'continuing education' and 'post-initial education'. Some of these phrases are associated with different policy aims. For example, the OECD term 'recurrent education' was originally associated with two objectives: to achieve a more equitable distribution of educational resources between the younger and older generations, and to reduce the gap between theory and practice, between students and workers. In later OECD reports, equality of educational and social opportunity gained priority over considerations of productivity and efficiency; the opportunity for active and creative participation in a decentralized and democratic society was stressed, in line with the Council of Europe's conception of the role of 'education permanente', and UNESCO's view of the place of 'lifelong learning'. By contrast the term 'post-initial education' was designed simply to indicate the time at which the student enters higher and further education. The even simpler phrase 'adult education' has come to mean principally non-vocational provision, and in this sense 'adult education' is often contrasted with 'continuing education', by which is then meant vocational provision. Here, however (as is defined at greater length later), 'continuing education' means all types of educational provision, after a break, for those outside the normal age range and stages of continuous initial education. Thus a new graduate embarking immediately on postgraduate work would not fall within the meaning of the term, but another 22-year-old, studying for GCE 'O' levels six years after leaving school would (see Propositions 2.1 and 3.2).

Proposition 1.1   An adequate approach to continuing education requires a shift in focus from the institution to the student.

Although the term 'continuing education' is neutral, in terms of policy objectives the implications of introducing an adequate provision for continuing education are quite fundamental, for they imply a shift in focus from the institution to the student — from, so to speak, education to learning (see Proposition 3.2). Adequate provision of continuing education implies a structure in which an adult can study at a level, at a time, and at a place appropriate to his or her own needs; and can study any subject or subjects in which he or she is interested, whether as part of a systematic course leading to some recognized qualification or certifiable increment of skill, or as a matter of personal development and enrichment. Clearly an educational system organized to permit, and encourage adults to use, such freedom will require profound institutional change; equally clearly the roles of universities and polytechnics in such a system will be partial, though crucial (see Propositions 2.6 and 3 passim). Only a small proportion of the adult population will want to study at a level to which these higher education institutions can appropriately respond — though even a small proportion may be a very large absolute number — and of these, again, only a small proportion will want to proceed to a degree. (There is a danger that in criticizing universities, for example, for failing adequately to provide for part-time students seeking a degree, enthusiasts for continuing education may fall into exactly the same restrictive frame of mind of which they accuse universities — viz. implying that the only *proper* continuing education student is one studying for a degree — though part-time!)

Proposition 1.2   An educational system adequate to the needs of continuing education will be, above all, open to student needs. The student will have adequate purchasing power and adequate guidance.

What characterizes an educational system adapted to the needs of continuing education is, to put it shortly, *openness*: the needs of the student are of primary importance. Ideally, the student should have *adequate purchasing power* — whether in the form of cash or vouchers — which can be exercised when desired over a lifetime (see Propositions 3.10 and 4.4). Adequate information and guidance are also essential (see Propositions 3.5 and 4.2). More controversially, this may lead to *competition* between providers, at least in some sectors.

Proposition 1.3   The higher education system has provided some continuing education for more than a century; but opportunities for development have been missed. The main obstacle is in attitudes.

Bits of the education system already exhibit at least some of the required characteristics — indeed, some have done so for a very long time. But the present piecemeal development and haphazard arrangements fall well short of what is desirable. In higher education, for example, over a century ago university extra-mural departments made possible the serious study by adults of difficult subjects, often under the direction of distinguished and inspiring teachers. Yet radical schemes which would have turned University Extension into a genuine open university, granting degrees, came to nothing, as Marriott's recent study, *A Backstairs to a Degree*, shows. The joint tutorial classes tradition ushered in by the foundation of the WEA was in one sense a further move towards a system of continuing education, in that it meant more power for the students; but in other respects it was a move away, in its denial of the value of certification and in its hostility towards more vocational motives and subjects for study.

Institutional change is needed to realize the comprehensive provision of continuing education. But the most profound changes required are in attitudes (see Propositions 2.2 and 3.7) and so in course regulations (see Propositions 2.6, 3.8 and 3.9), rather than in buildings: they are, therefore, relatively inexpensive. Why, then, have they not been adopted hitherto, and what is the justification for making them now?

The Economy of Educational Spending

Proposition 1.4   There are large disparities in the resources allocated to full-time and part-time students and, in the part-time sector, between vocational and non-vocational study.

The statistics on enrolments in and resources devoted to continuing education in Great Britain are notoriously inadequate. A recent study by Maureen Woodhall, *The Scope and Costs of the Education and Training of Adults in Britain,* commissioned by ACACE, suggests that between five and six million adults are at present engaged in some form of education or training each year — that is between one-third and one-half of the number engaged in formal initial education. The expenditure on this education and training for adults, which is largely part-time, is *probably less than half* that devoted to the initial full-time education system. This picture is broadly comparable with that which obtained around 1970. The broad comparison of costs and numbers is rather misleading, however, for within continuing education there is a great disparity between the resources available for vocational and non-vocational courses. Vocational education and training tends to be inherently more expensive than non-vocational. Hence a vocational part-time student costs roughly twenty times as much as a non-vocational. So far as can be ascertained, this discrepancy has not changed much since 1970 either.

There are *two main economic reasons for concentration of systematic educational resources on the young.* The first is that up to a certain point the benefits to society as a whole from initial education far outweigh the benefits which accrue to the individual. It is important for society that its individual members should be literate and numerate so as to be effective as workers of whatsoever kind and so as to be able to communicate with one another and to share certain patterns of thought and codes of conduct. The earlier these lessons can be learned, the greater the proportion of any given society which will be able to maintain the society, to communicate and to behave in socially beneficial ways. And many of the lessons can be learned best when minds are young and uncluttered. The second reason is closely related: if education is regarded as an example of what economists call 'investment in human capital', the earlier the investment is undertaken the longer the stream of returns to that capital investment — in the form of extra output made possible by the skills acquired. Further, the loss of output incurred whilst education is taking place is smaller the younger the student (see Proposition 2.2).

Technology, Demography and Inequalities

Proposition 1.5   Rapid technological development both demands regular updating and creates more leisure. These are the two 'main' grounds for transferring resources to continuing or post-initial education.

Although both the above reasons provide an economic justification for education expenditure in the early years of life, they cannot indicate how much should be spent. And if the 'investment' undertaken in the early years suffers from depreciation and, even worse, becomes obsolete, replacement (refresher courses) and new investment in more modern technology (up-dating or retraining courses) are essential. The *speed and scope of technical progress nowadays supplies the first main argument in favour of allotting a substantial proportion of educational resources to later in a student's lifetime*, though initial education must still be funded to fulfil the role described in the paragraph above. When technical progress was relatively slow it was reasonable to conceive of the labour force adapting to it by slow changes in the schools' curriculum: thus each successive cohort released from initial education into the labour force had skills which were adapted to current technology. As the speed of technical progress increased and its scope became wider the education system adapted by lengthening the initial education process, and devoting proportionately more and more resources to the higher and further levels of initial education. Many observers argue that *the technical progress we now face is of a quite different order* from that hitherto experienced — as fundamental as the industrial revolution but much quicker to spread. If the industrial revolution involved the invention of devices which extended human muscles, the electronic revolution extends the human nervous system. In the information technology society, it has been said, the only insurance against future shock is to educate for a changing future. And although this will obviously have implications for initial education — perhaps in reasserting the importance of a good grasp of basic principles and of a quick and adaptable cast of mind — its most important implication is for continuing education. Frequent job changes and the education for them will become crucial.

The notion that teaching adults is outside the normal remit of institutions of higher education will, in these circumstances, rapidly come to seem absurd. Already few would regard postgraduate clinical medical education, designed to keep doctors' techniques up to date, as outside the 'proper' role of a university: it is a natural outlet for the university's research. As the pace of technological change grows, it will be in continuing education courses, as much as at the postgraduate level, that researchers will find their natural channel of communication (see Propositions 2.6 and 3.3).

The second main reason for devoting more resources to continuing education *is the combination of such technical change with demographic factors.* The potential labour force is expanding whilst technical change is reducing the demand for labour. Even if we avoid the simultaneous inflationary and deflationary consequences of periodic increases in oil prices, the demand for labour will be sluggish. Increased leisure time will be available, whether by design (in planned reductions in the working week), or involuntarily (through unemployment). Some critics dismiss continuing education offered and undertaken in such circumstances as a mere agent of social control; but the imaginative use of the time freed by the advance of technology to allow students to explore knowledge in all its forms, to use information, to formulate, plan and execute community initiatives freely and openly — in short, to learn to live and act within a democracy — must be viewed as an enormous potential enrichment of the individual and of society. We are reminded of Bacon's definition of the purposes of knowledge: 'For the love of God and the relief of man's estate'.

The third reason for promoting continuing education is as valid in a period of rapid and uncertain change as it was a century ago in a period of steady, confident growth — namely, *to distribute some educational resources later to compensate for the inequitable initial distribution.* The heavy incidence of unemployment amongst the poorly educated is a striking example of the necessity to promote opportunities for study after the initial, often unhappy, education phase is completed (see Proposition 3.10).

Proposition 1.6 *The use of continuing education to remedy earlier educational disadvantages is less acknowledged than its use in providing advanced further training.*

Professor A.H. Halsey has pointed out that there is a basic conflict between continuing education aimed at assimilating or reacting to technical progress and continuing education as a means of advancement for the educationally deprived. In the first case continuing education is often a 'positional' good — it helps an already well-educated part of the labour force to hold onto its advantage through its facility in using advanced techniques. But in its redistributive role continuing education seeks to erode positional advantage by substituting later instruction for earlier deficiencies in education. The resolution of this conflict is to be sought by ensuring that the continuing education provision is widely defined and widely based within each institution, and does not concentrate exclusively on either refresher or remedial work.

A Short-Term, Short-Sighted Approach
Professional, vocationally-oriented, short courses seem particularly appealing in present circumstances, when higher and further education seeks to minimize the impact of cuts in long-standing sources of central funding by earning money from the private sector. Although the expansion of such provision is to be welcomed, it is not by itself an adequate response to the need for an adequate range of continuing education. The task facing us is to harness the economic pressures which are forcing institutions into more continuing education activity, and to use them to reform the institutions themselves so that each according to its nature and strengths expresses and fulfils a wide definition of continuing education. The next two sections consider the present position and what changes should take place.

STAFF AND STUDENTS: ATTITUDES AND DEMANDS

The Present Situation

Proposition 2.1   Continuing education caters for all adults undertaking formal or non-formal study, full- or part-time, at any level and at any time after the completion of, and after the break from, their initial education at, and immediately following, school.

There might be ground for asserting that Britain already has more higher education than it needs, or at least more than it can afford. But that would be an economic rather than an educational argument, and like most economic arguments would remain open to different if not contrary interpretations. There is equally an economic case — which has been made in the preceding section — for improving the educational competence of the whole population. Given that higher education is the magnet which shapes the pattern of the rest of the educational system, its scale and scope are critical both to the provision of initial education and to that of post-initial or continuing education. Hence, if continuing education is to develop, we need to be clear where higher education stands at present in relation to the education of adults. Is it dealing adequately with adults' educational needs and demands, and if not — why not?

In primary and secondary schooling it is reasonable to regard the students as children. In higher education the student body is not so clearly defined. Physically and psychologically at least, the students can be regarded as adults, but there is also an educational distinction to be drawn. Most higher education students are finishing their education direct from school — they are completing their initial education. It is only a much smaller proportion who have completed their initial education and have then returned to higher education. They are the ones who have decided to continue their education as adults; or, for want of a more elegant term, they form the post-initial or continuing education sector. How far therefore does the higher education system provide for them (see Proposition 1.1)?

Attitudes and Responses

Proposition 2.2   Staff attitudes are too much dominated by the 'front-end model' of education.

The general public's attitude to education is that it is for the young. It is a finite (and compulsory) experience from which most of the population gratefully escape as soon as the minimum school-leaving age is reached — and for the most part they never return to formal education. Education is in effect no longer on the adult agenda. It is no surprise therefore that many school teachers share this attitude, or at least recognize its pervasiveness and force; hence the pressures on the school curriculum to fit in as much as possible, and sometimes more, in order to complete the pupils' education. Similarly, staff in higher education see their main job as completing the education of those young people who are regarded — through the examination system — as able to benefit from higher education.

Thus the 'front-end model' of loading the young with their full complement of educational stores to sustain them through life dominates the whole educational system and influences the attitudes of very many educators. This influence is strengthened by the fact that most teachers and educational administrators, particularly in higher education, are themselves the 'successes' of this system and regard themselves as having an obligation to help others succeed in the same way. This is where educators are in a sense in the business of reproducing their own educational experiences. In itself this cannot be objected to, but it is a matter for concern when the conventional educational route assumes such importance that any other road is rated as no more than a by-way.

Educators' familiarity with the front-end model inevitably leads many of them to regard the relatively few adult students with whom they come into contact as rarities or eccentrics. In one sense of course they are: they are at least unconventional in entering higher education outside the usual and restricted age range and sometimes without the normal entry requirements. For teachers adult students are much less easy to categorize, much less easy to predict and to assess in their range of prior knowledge and experience. They can create an atmosphere quite distinct from the relative homogeneity of a class full of young adults coming direct from school.

Thus adult students can call for different approaches from their teachers and this may be felt to be an additional burden in the accustomed teaching routine, especially when adult students form only a very small proportion of those being taught. In practice many teachers come to appreciate and even make use of the presence of adult attitudes and experience in their classes, but it can take time to recognize this as a ready-made 'teaching aid'; and the early encounters with adult students can be disturbing, particularly for young teachers when they meet the adult auto-didacts who are ready to do battle with a received wisdom which does not match their own experience.

There is a circular effect at work here. Staff in higher education are familiar with their part in the initial education system, both from their own student days and from their expectation of what is required of them when they join or succeed their own teachers. This experience has confirmed that their job is to prepare young people for life. Adult students have scarcely figured in that experience; it can therefore be very difficult to appreciate why they should now do so, and even more difficult to know how they should be coped with. To break this circle we need more adult students in higher education, but their entry is largely dependent on the very attitudes which have drawn the circle (see Proposition 3.7).

Proposition 2.3   Historically, academic drift has often led to (i) a reduction in the provision and status of part-time and preparatory lower-level work; (ii) excessive concentration on 18-plus full-time students.

The phrase 'academic drift', originally coined by Tyrrell Burgess, indicates the apparently inescapable process in British higher education which continually leads educational institutions to seek higher status by copying the manners of those institutions above them in the educational league table. Drift may not be a sufficiently purposeful word to describe the ways in which, for example, early nineteenth-century mechanic institutes have climbed the institutional ladder to become late twentieth-century universities, but the process and its effects are evident enough. Many institutions which began by providing part-time, generally evening, study opportunities for, chiefly, working-class adults, often at elementary levels of instruction, have been transformed into centres of full-time study, at degree or comparable levels, for predominantly middle-class young adults. Educational status, for staff and students, lies in full-time and higher-level study. The price which has frequently been paid is the abandonment of part-time study facilities and lower-level work. This has been both required and encouraged by Britain's pre-eminent record in providing mandatory student awards for specified courses of full-time study. The consequent result has been still further concentration on provision for geographically mobile young adults without domestic responsibilities, to the relative exclusion of adults. In this way what are almost institutional instincts have combined with individual staff attitudes to reinforce the view that full-time initial education is the principal and virtually exclusive purpose of higher education.

Proposition 2.4   Expansion in the 1960s was a missed opportunity.

It is now apparent that the enormous development of higher education in the 1960s did not prompt any considerable move to extend its benefits to a wider range of students. The Robbins principle of making higher education available to all who were willing and able to benefit from it was actively responded to — by providing more of the same forms of study to very many more of the same kinds of students. Whether this move has led to worse standards is a matter for debate, but it has certainly not led to proportionately more provision for adult students.

The form of provision has remained predominantly full-time and its adherence to closely defined academic disciplines, linked to equally well-defined school examinations, has continued — with the exception of limited excursions into interdisciplinary studies. There has been an understandable concern to maintain academic standards, but this too has contributed to a blinkered view of possible new developments which the vast growth of student numbers might have encouraged. Very few universities have made positive or well-advertised efforts to attract a wider age range of students, as Table 2.1 illustrates.

In the universities continuing education has remained the province of the extra-mural departments, and though their work has grown it has remained marginal to the main concerns and resource allocation of the universities. Very little progress has been made in extending extra-mural provision into the heartland of university teaching at degree level. The splendid exception here is the Open University, but it could be argued that the opening of the OU has made the other universities even more disinclined to develop part-time first degree work.

Some polytechnics and a few institutes of higher education have made positive efforts to attract adult students, and they have been helped and encouraged in this by the liberal attitudes of the Council for National

TABLE 2.1
Full-time/sandwich home undergraduate new entrants to United Kingdom universities by age (Thousands: column percentages in brackets)

	1971/72	1979/80
20 and under	55.1 (86.7)	68.6 (87.0)
21-24	5.5 (8.6)	5.7 (7.2)
25 and over	2.9 (4.6)	4.5 (5.7)
Total	63.6 (100.0)	78.9 (100.0)
Total 21 and over	8.5 (13.3)	10.2 (13.0)

Source
Fulton 1981, p. 154

Academic Awards towards entry requirements. But the pull of academic drift has been strong and the ever present desire to enhance academic status has militated against any widespread moves to attract initially less well-qualified adult students onto courses adapted and timetabled to their requirements. The study by Malcolm Tight, *Part-time Degree Level Study in the United Kingdom* (Tight 1982), shows among other things how limited is the supply.

One area which has grown noticeably over recent years in universities and polytechnics is in post-experience courses, designed mainly for adults who seek to improve their knowledge and skills in mid-career. The Department of Education and Science has shown a welcome interest in encouraging this growth: it may be hoped that it will not be too long in taking some practical initiatives arising from its 1980 discussion paper on 'Continuing Education', limited though that was to 'post experience vocational provision for those in employment'. But it would certainly be regrettable if the higher education system regarded continuing education as no more than that.

Proposition 2.5   There is every reason to suppose that there is a substantial latent demand.

One may advocate the development of continuing education, but there is no easy way of demonstrating the size of the demand for it. No doubt many higher education institutions would respond more adequately to the needs of adult students if those students were to make their educational demands known. Supply would follow demand. But educational needs are difficult to translate into specific demands, and even when those demands can be clearly expressed they are only likely to be presented to institutions which are already known to be making an appropriate supply. Potential adult students find it difficult to know what they want until they know what they can have. Demand therefore follows supply.

This has been dramatically illustrated by the Open University. In the late 1960s the planners of the OU were anxious about the likely size of the demand for part-time degree study. None of the conventional universities had evidence of unsatisfied demand for part-time study, but then almost none of them offered that kind of study. In the event the OU admissions list has been oversubscribed every year, with two or more applicants for each available place. Thus the supply of part-time degree study has revealed the previously unexpressed need for it and transformed that need into a measurable demand.

One way of indicating possible unsatisfied demand is through national comparisons. As shown in Table 2.2, the Advisory Council for Adult and Continuing Education (ACACE) presented evidence to the House of Commons Select Committee on Education, Science and the Arts which compared the number of undergraduate students as a percentage of total national populations in the UK with three other industrially developed countries in the late 1970s. The results suggest that the UK may still have a substantial unsatisfied demand for first degree study.

TABLE 2.2
National comparisons — numbers of undergraduate students as percentage of total national population

Country	Total national population	Total undergraduate population	Undergraduate population as % of total national population
USA	210 millions	8,053,000	3.83%
Sweden	8 millions	157,305	1.97%
Canada	25 millions	490,740	1.96%
UK	56 millions	358,277	0.64%

It may be no coincidence that the United States has the most highly developed educational advisory services for adults. These, in addition to giving information and advice on suitable courses, act as 'brokers' between institutions and potential students to transmit two-way information about supply and demand. This helps institutions to find out about demand and respond to it, and helps students to negotiate access to the existing supply. Britain has very few of these services and they are nearly all operated on the smallest of budgets (see 1979 ACACE report, *Links to Learning*) (see Proposition 4.2).

It is certainly no coincidence that the USA and Canada have massive provision for part-time study at undergraduate level. This allows them to provide for large numbers of part-time students in a way which is very largely denied to adults in Britain.

Before concluding this part of the chapter with a brief look at part-time study provision, it needs to be noted that evidence is beginning to accumulate on the latent and actual demand for education by adults. An ACACE national survey of adults' educational experience and needs, based on interviews with 2,500 people, is to be published in 1982. This shows that 23 per cent of the adult population had undertaken some kind of formal education or training in the previous three years, and 61 per cent indicated some area of interest which they would like to study if the opportunity (mostly part-time study) presented itself. Out of the total sample, 3 per cent mentioned an interest in working for a degree and a further 7 per cent mentioned other qualifications: these percentages may seem small, but 3 per cent of the adult population over the age of twenty-one is a million people.

Thus there seems to be every reason to believe that there is a very large number of adults able and willing to continue their education, and a still more substantial number looking to higher education for this opportunity.

Proposition 2.6   Part-time study is a main key to new developments in higher education.

Most adults have domestic responsibilities, jobs and incomes which they are understandably reluctant to sacrifice in order to continue their education full-time. Yet so many of the educational opportunities available to them are full-time, often over quite lengthy periods of time, and are therefore only accessible by making great sacrifices. Thus many adults are denied the chance of formal study in higher education, although part-time study — with the students still gainfully employed and not needing student awards and residential accommodation — could be an excellent investment for the national exchequer.

Comparisons can be made with Canada, whose higher education institutions have English and Scottish antecedents, where 35 per cent of the undergraduate enrolments in 1978-79 were part-time (174,000 out of a total of 316,000). One concomitant of this (although other political, economic and social factors apply) is that only 25 per cent of students

TABLE 2.3
Part-time undergraduates, United Kingdom, 31 December 1976

	Part-time Undergraduates			All undergraduates	Part-time undergraduates as % of all undergraduates
	(1) Male	(2) Female	(3) Total	(4) Total	(5) (3) as % of (4)
Universities	1,944	1,868	3,812	232,081	1.6%
Polytechnics (England and Wales)	3,391	799	4,190	75,161	5.6%
Open University	30,635	20,400	51,035	51,035	100%
Total	35,970	23,067	59,037	358,277	16.5%

Source
DES 'Statistics of Education 1979' and OU 'Digest of Statistics 1971-78'.

in Canadian higher education receive government financial aid compared with 90 per cent in the UK.

There is clearly enormous scope for the development of part-time study in British higher education. The Open University has shown the way and Flexistudy is beginning to prove that part-time learning at a distance is also attractive to students in further education. Distance learning needs to be taken much more seriously by higher education institutions. But it is only one form of part-time study. An increase in conventional face-to-face teaching in the evenings and at weekends could draw on the local adult population within reach of higher education institutes, particularly those adults who are reluctant or unprepared to study at a distance (see Proposition 3.3).

These developments will call for organizational changes, including some of importance in modular courses, credit transfer and entry requirements (see Propositions 3.8 and 3.9). Just as importantly, we shall need to encourage shifts in institutional and individual staff attitudes if the familiar shape of higher education is to be adapted to the demands and the benefits of continuing education.

WHAT SHOULD BE DONE?

Premises, Co-operation, Contracts of Service
As has already been hinted, the greatest problem inhibiting the fuller

development of continuing education within the higher education sector is the conservatism of human nature. Why do a majority of British first degree programmes last three years? Because they have traditionally been of that length. Why will fresh forms of continuing education only be accepted with great caution? Because they represent something new, if not in type at least in proposed quantity. These objectives are usually presented as the protection of academic standards and sometimes this is a fair claim. Just as often the motive is a rooted disinclination to change; higher education, as the most prestigious sector of education and thus one which fears it has most to lose by change, is predictably the most conservative area of educational provision.

Proposition 3.1   The type of higher education normally available during the day should also be provided during evenings and weekends.

Some obvious barriers to the wider provision of continuing education within higher education arise from problems of time and space. Most institutions of higher education in Britain shape their provision to the needs of full-time students who attend only during the day. To the institutions this is attractive since it is convenient. Its disadvantage is that it cuts off almost all the adult population from the higher education resources provided by the community. Yet in 1981 the Open University received almost 25 per cent more inquiries about its first degree courses than in 1980, and that sort of growth is not new. Despite such indicators, and there are others, most higher education institutions continue to ignore the difficulties of access for those who are in full-time employment or are housebound because of having young children or some disability. Until institutions more often recognize that there are other potential students than 18-year-olds with a grant for three years of full-time study, continuing education will be sorely inhibited.

An obvious first move would be to make available during the evenings and at weekends what is normally provided within each institution during the day. A modest number of such programmes exist already, most notably at Birkbeck College within the University of London; and there are institutions such as Goldsmiths' College, also within the University of London, and Trent Polytechnic which provide some of their first degrees in both full-time and part-time versions. Studying for higher degrees by part-time registration has proved more acceptable to the institutions of higher education than has part-time study for first degrees. Similarly, there is some sympathy for increasing the provision of part-time post-experience courses. The present climate is less sympathetic to the expansion of so-called non-vocational short courses in part-time programmes.

As has been argued above (p. 39), the vast majority of institutions of higher education still think of themselves as overwhelmingly for full-time students, even though they may in fact have very many part-time students.

For example, the University of Nottingham has some 6,000 full-time students. It has far more part-time students, such as the 11,000 in its extra-mural programme, or the 3,000 in post-experience courses in the Faculty of Education, or the substantial number of part-time higher degree students, or those taking the courses put on by the Industrial and Business Liasion Office, or those recruited through the initiatives of individual departments. Such programmes, found in most institutions of higher education, have resulted from the insistent demand for continuing education from the general public. Despite such evidence, a majority of institutions would claim that they are before all else bodies for full-time undergraduate study. The ad hoc nature of their continuing education provision, large though it may sometimes be, results from their unwillingness to recognize that change is already in train. The increasing pressure for continuing education programmes makes their belief that they should provide nothing much more than full-time study dangerously limiting. Because of a variety of changes already under way in British society there is a need for all institutions of higher education to see various forms of part-time provision as at least as important as their full-time programmes.

Proposition 3.2   Every community with reasonable access to an institution of higher education should have its own centre suitably equipped for use by adult students. Such provision will have both professional and academic implications for staff.

Tied up with the key issue of part-time provision is that of buildings. Whilst the Open University has demonstrated great success in providing courses largely through a system of correspondence education, with some use of television and radio (or perhaps of study centres), many would-be students seek a continuing education based on face-to-face teaching. Such students have already highlighted the inadequacy for adults of buildings designed for 18-year-olds. Often they lack several kinds of facility needed by adult students; and hardly any have crèches. The higher education campus is frequently in an inconvenient place several miles from the city centre; the British tradition of residential higher education and the somewhat medieval view of desirable locations for universities have made the geographical location of particular universities eccentric with regard to population distribution. Small towns such as Colchester and Canterbury have universities whilst large towns such as Derby do not. In some instances large towns with universities have relocated them in new campuses away from their nineteenth-century, city centre, original sites.

Such factors suggest the need for outlying centres. Academics should expect to find themselves following the long-established extra-mural tradition of travelling to classes off campus. For example, it would seem sensible for a member of the Faculty of Engineering to teach, for part of a course, within a factory where the engineers seeking post-experience tuition are to be found. Similarly it would appear unreasonable to expect evening students to travel substantial distances to a campus if they are within a town where there is enthusiasm enough to support a class. Every community at a distance from an institution of higher education should have a centre for higher education suitably equipped for use by adult students. Some universities, through their extra-mural departments, already have such centres (for example Nottingham University with its centres at Boston, Derby, Loughborough, Matlock, Nottingham (since the university campus is three miles from the city centre), and Lincoln). In short, an increase in the provision of continuing education implies the development of many centres outside the higher education campuses and the acceptance that a lecturer's life should be partly peripatetic. Often the resources for creating such higher education centres away from the campus already exist in embryo; for example, the empty schools or classrooms made available by a declining birthrate. Though such accommodation would need careful conversion to suit the needs of adults, the capital resources called for would be relatively modest. Perhaps more difficult would be persuading higher education teaching staff to make available their professional skills off-campus.

In continuing education the needs of the students have a special importance and the wishes of the teachers, except where founded in good academic principles rather than in the convenience of the higher education institution itself, must be secondary. Such a focus will cause considerable discomfort in some instances; for example, higher education staffs have become more and more specialized, and yet the needs of adult students are frequently interdisciplinary. Inter-departmental co-operation will need to develop; history again suggests that this will be difficult to achieve because of the conservatism of academics. Throughout this chapter, it will be seen repeatedly, the most challenging issue is that of the attitudes of those involved. There is a need for more hospitable educationalists and for a greater awareness amongst the adult population as to what may properly be asked of the higher education system (see Proposition 1.1)

Proposition 3.3   There is a need for greater co-operation between educational and other institutions in the provision of continuing education.

As well as inadequate co-operation within institutions there is a history of poor co-operation between institutions. There is a class system amongst institutions not wholly to be justified on academic grounds, so that, for example, universities are seen as at the top of the pile, whilst polytechnics look down on the institutes of higher education. In an age when there is an increasing need in providing for adults for effective co-operation between, say, local authority further education colleges and higher education institutions within the private sector, old assumptions about a pecking order may get in the way. The more recently published Sheffield study on *Mature Students in Further and Higher Education* (University of Sheffield 1981) does much to prove that a greater integration of further and higher education is called for. Since institutions providing both higher and further education still lie largely in the future there is a need for effective local, regional and national co-operation between institutions to meet the needs of continuing education during the rest of this century. Such predictable developments as permanent and increasing unemployment and rapid technological and social change make the old boundary lines outdated. Those examples of inter-institutional co-operation already in being need to be reinforced by a review of existing machinery, such as the Regional Advisory Councils for Further Education, with a view to its streamlining and supplementation. As is so often the case, a number of administrative bodies have come into being in the typical British ad hoc way. They have been responses to particular situations. One might ask, for example, whether the future of continuing education would be best served by the integration of the Universities Council for Adult and Continuing Education with the National Institute of Adult Education. Other local and national examples will come readily to mind. If resources are scarce, effective institutional co-operation in the provision of continuing education has a pressing urgency. Institutions of higher education cannot continue to be the narrow, inward-looking societies they have so often been.

Other forms of co-operation will need to be developed or extended. Many institutions, particularly those in the public sector of higher education, have a good record of co-operation with employers. This should be built on. Since we are already in an age of 'information crisis' with its related need for up-dating, all higher education institutions must improve on their record of association with outside bodies. The sort of co-operation a good school of education within a university has with its local education authorities, in which there is continuous negotiation over the post-experience needs of schoolteachers, administrators, school governors and others, is to be recommended. It is worth noting that a large number of the resulting courses are taught by professionals from the education service. The higher education institution acts as the organizing agency. This also makes available to the institution new knowledge not to be found within its own ranks. Among the advantages of the autonomy enjoyed by higher education, as against the disadvantages already noted, is this: such institutions provide an attractive forum for people from other professional areas and have a reputation for 'neutrality'. Sensitive topics can be discussed and developed which cannot be so easily handled in other arenas. A firm's industrial relations officer may feel better able to discuss his field fully and frankly as a tutor of a polytechnic continuing education course than as a teacher in a company programme. Even if this is not always true, there is no doubt that the interchange of staff between institutions of higher education and outside organizations enriches both. Further incentives should be found to ensure a substantial increase in such co-operation within continuing education. There are a number of existing models ranging from those within the National Health Service to those schemes for seconding schoolteachers to industry. There needs to be more awareness of what has already been done, and greater national co-ordination.

Another area of co-operation is that between institutions of higher education and the broadcasting agencies. Since continuing education is likely to be the main area of growth in education as the 1980s pass, broadcasters should be even more involved in developing the potentialities of radio and television in this area. The responsibilities and role of the broadcasting agencies in continuing education should be explicitly reaffirmed. Such exhortations will not achieve much unless there are more professionals on both sides with a brief for continuing education. Institutions of higher education should give specific members of staff a broadcasting liaison brief. Within the broadcasting agencies educationalists appointed within the most senior professional ranks could eventually form an effective lobby. In spite of reassurances from the broadcasters, most people in continuing education have yet to be convinced that broadcasting fully reflects the importance of their field of work. That sense will only be ensured when there are as many links as possible, at as many levels as are available between the broadcasters and the institutions of continuing education.

Since resources for continuing education are unlikely to grow at the speed of demand, the time and space barriers to effective provision have to be tackled effectively. Education will always have fewer resources than it feels it needs, so those resources will have to be made even more effective. Traditionally, thorny problems have been avoided or only partly challenged. There has been hostility to the pooling of institutional resources, a 'priesthood' attitude to the use of resources from outside the educational system, a reluctance to accept that part-time students are as important as full-timers. As we have seen, present trends suggest that the time may be coming when most institutions of higher education will see themselves as primarily part-time student agencies. We should be planning now for such developments.

Proposition 3.4   Contracts for new academic staff should be broadly based and include a formal commitment to continuing education.

It would greatly aid the adjustment of the field of higher education to the changes underway if new staff contracts were more broadly based and included a formal commitment to continuing education. Many areas of education, such as further education, already assume that staff contracts will call for work in the evenings and at weekends. Despite the existence for many years of full-time extra-mural staff, 'unsocial hours' of teaching such as theirs are not easily accepted elsewhere within the higher education sector. Each institution would need to review the contracts of its existing staff, but it would seem particularly necessary to have a clear commitment to continuing education teaching built into all new staff contracts. It is to be hoped that a contract stating that up to a certain percentage of teaching time could be devoted to continuing education would produce a new generation of higher education tutors who assume that it is as 'normal' to teach adults in the evening as undergraduates by day. This would recognize the initial problem of, in some cases, divided loyalties. Because of present assumptions within institutions of higher education most staff will initially see themselves as primarily teachers of full-time undergraduates and only a few will see themselves as more strongly committed to continuing education. Despite such attitudes, justice should and can be done to both.

Proposition 3.5 *The professional development of teachers should include training for work with students in continuing education*

To accelerate a fair deal for continuing education the training of staff in the field will need to be extended. Despite a number of reports, ranging from that of the Advisory Committee on the Supply and Training of Teachers to the Universities Council for Adult and Continuing Education, the training of teachers within institutions of higher education in the tutoring of adults has been much less impressive than that found amongst the part-time teachers within the local education authorities' adult education service. Most academics seem to feel that they need no training to teach, despite their belief in very lengthy training for research. To return to a familiar theme: the first stage of any debate on training is to break down the traditional higher education attitudes to improving teaching.

In the past, teachers in higher education have had largely uncritical audiences, as is reported in the Sheffield Study already referred to (p. 49). Mature students were consistently more critical of what were considered to be poor lectures, seminars or tutorials than were the conventional students. It was a surprise to many of the older students that the 18-year-old entrants appeared unwilling to contribute to discussion or to question values or assumptions, and that they seemed prepared to sit in silence, to take notes obediently and apparently to accept everything that was said. Mature students both in the university and the polytechnic regarded informal discussions with staff and with other students as 'necessary and valuable' learning experiences, but at the same time they believed their lecturers had little confidence in the value of such discussions.

The first stage in any discussion about training for teaching in the education of adults will largely consist in breaking down hostility to the proposal itself. Most surveys among higher education staff suggest at best an indifference to training-for-teaching programmes, and in many instances an aggressive opposition. In no institutions is such training seen as remotely as important as having a PhD in your subject area. The time may nonetheless come when all those teaching in higher education will be obliged to have a professional teaching qualification as do schoolteachers. Given present financial restraints, such a time is still far off. In the meantime the rapid development of continuing education suggests that poor teaching — often accepted in full-time education — will be less and less tolerated.

The long established extra-mural departments of universities usually have training schemes for their part-time tutors. These provide in most instances one or two evening and weekend meetings and some advice on each subject area. The department's full-time tutors usually visit the new tutor in class and there is some useful printed material. This bare minimum is the very least that should be provided for a tutor about to take a class of adults for the first time. When many local education authorities now send their new part-time teachers to teach their first class only after a minimum of thirty hours of preparation, the more amateur approach of institutions of higher education seems even less acceptable.

Those in continuing education will be faced by the particular learning needs of a wide range of people, from youngsters with school experience still in their minds to adults who have been away from educational institutions for forty years or so. Adult students are heterogeneous and, rightly, demanding. Their experience may well make them in some respects shrewder and better informed than their tutors. They represent a much greater challenge than the normal undergraduate class. Such continuing education groups will expect effective teaching. It seems an obvious point to make, but training in teaching adults really is likely to improve tutoring. A growth in continuing education must be accompanied by a comprehensive network of tutor training schemes.

Curricula, Teaching Methods, Selection

Proposition 3.6   Curricula should be more flexible, so as to suit adult needs.

There is always a danger that institutions of higher education, in seeking to meet the increased demand for continuing education, will merely make available their present full-time programme in a part-time format. But it is a common experience in teaching adults that the students are often disinclined to fit into existing subject lines and that they expect disciplines to be more flexible than most academics have been willing to accept. Their wider questioning of curricula goes beyond the conventional boundaries between disciplines. Tutors of adults need to take a much more open view of the curricula and to be open to often naïve but yet central questions. Courses in physics may end up by also reviewing the role of science in contemporary society; a programme in local history might find itself dealing with a community's concept of the good life at different periods. Ignoring such challenges to the established curricula will do less than justice to the students and miss an opportunity to encourage the tutor to review his own work. Such subject flexibility must not compromise the intellectual demands made of students and teachers.

Some courses for adults should be problem-based rather than discipline-based. In that most difficult of fields from the adult student's viewpoint, physics, the former extra-mural tutor Sam Lilley has written a text entitled *Discovering Relativity for Yourself* (Cambridge University Press 1980). He writes of his experience:

> 'I introduced Relativity amongst my courses in 1958. And since then I have been teaching it to carpenters and clerks, housewives, miners and insurance agents — to all sorts of people who have no special qualifications for learning the subject and others like teachers and professional engineers who have limited qualifications. At first I taught it badly. But the customs of the Adult Education world enabled me to learn by my mistakes. Discussion bulks large in my classes. Students are encouraged to raise their difficulties and argue about them — till I find how to get them past the barriers. They are encouraged to argue back — try to prove Einstein (and me) wrong. They must be genuinely convinced before we move on. How much (or little) my students learned from the earlier classes I do not know. But I learned an immense amount. Amid these discussions and arguments I came to understand that their main difficulties were not the ones that might reasonably be anticipated. Nor were they the ones that could be dealt with by mere logical explanations. They needed a more roundabout approach. So I developed the practice of tape-recording every class, listening to the playback, analysing students' problems, spotting my deficiencies, and keeping systematic notes of all this. From autumn 1963 to spring 1970 I did this for every Relativity course I took — a total of 650 hours of recordings, and maybe 2,000 or more hours of playback.'

Dr Lilley's book reveals how a talented tutor can take a most difficult subject and introduce it with great success to generations of supposedly unqualified adults. In the process he illustrates remarkable flexibility and an unusual degree of professional commitment. The result is greater enjoyment for the tutor, highly satisfied students, and a piece of educational innovation for anyone teaching physics, or any other subject, to any age group. There is little doubt that the arrival of increasing numbers of adult students at the various institutions of higher education will produce substantial innovations. If there is too much resistance to the subsequent redefinition of subjects the institutions and their staffs will be the major losers.

Proposition 3.7   Teachers must be receptive to new teaching methods.

Much has already been said about teaching methods for adults. Of these, Edward Hutchison (1963) wrote that they must take into account 'expressed and implied demands; the character and strength of motivation in relation to varying degrees of individual capacity; the extent and nature of previous education; the practical possibilities of time and place'. What is also often forgotten is the need for the tutor to assess his own strengths and weaknesses. To be sensitive to the students, but not to oneself, is only half the battle.

Whilst the teaching methods known to be effective with adults, namely 'relaxed' groups guided by a thoroughly knowledgeable tutor, willing to allow substantial relevant discussion, and whose class meetings are supplemented by plenty of reading and out-of-class written work, will serve the bulk of the continuing education demand, new methods are of increasing importance. The Open University has demonstrated how effective correspondence education can be. Distance learning is an effective way of reaching isolated students or those who wish to work on their own. A number of institutions of higher education might follow the example of Massey University in New Zealand or the University of New England in Australia and combine facilities which serve both a campus-based full-time undergraduate and a postgraduate student body with an extensive distance learning programme.

The arrival of the 'Open Tech' and the increasing acceptance of Flexistudy will increase and aid the adult student body. Much of the new technology has yet to be fully explored, let alone employed; word processors are a good example of an innovation with broad-ranging and yet barely realized implications for continuing education. Though most people seem to prefer face-to-face teaching, there is a need to explore such new areas as computer-aided education, floppy discs, and many other recent aids. Though teaching methods may in the event change less than is often claimed today, the need for an open-minded approach on the part of tutors will be important.

Proposition 3.8   A great range of acceptable selection criteria, such as experiential credits, should be explored.

So often adult students suffer from a lack of information, or from mis-information, about available educational opportunities. A number of reports, such as those of the Advisory Council for Adult and Continuing Education and the Association for Recurrent Education, have proposed better educational guidance and counselling services. A national and local network is obviously a pressing priority. If it were available, would-be adult students would not assume, for example, that entry to a first degree programme always demands at least two GCE 'A' levels. Many institutions of higher education already have schemes to accept 'unqualified' mature students for entry to first degree courses.

Whilst such examples of imaginative entry criteria are heartening they are not the norm. There should be a national agreement which encourages institutions of higher education to review their policies on entry to courses so as to allow for those ill-equipped with formal qualifications but with compensating experience of working life. Credits for experience, whether to waive entrance requirements or in place of course units, are used much less than they might be. Experience in employment, voluntary and public service and similar pursuits should be taken into account, as are formal qualifications. Claims that this will lead to a lowering of academic standards seem unwarranted, although mature students on first degree courses do seem to have a higher than average drop-out rate. The latter may partly result from most institutions being ill-suited to adult students' needs.

Some agency such as the Advisory Council for Adult and Continuing Education should explore acceptable alternatives to the various established qualifications for course entry. For instance, the flexible use of multiple selection criteria has much to recommend it. There is considerable experience to call upon, both abroad and in Britain (eg in industry and the armed forces). This should also encompass course credit for relevant experience and such related themes as 'credit entitlement'.

Flexibility, Finance, Research

Proposition 3.9   Wider acceptance of modular courses and credit transfer is needed.

The provision of continuing education is greatly aided by programmes built up of modular courses. These programmes are made up from separate units which part-time students can take without loss of continuity. Although there is some fear that the 'fragmentation' of programmes might lead to a curbing of curriculum innovation a recognition of this possibility should itself lead to action to avoid that side effect.

Ideally, an acceptance of modular course structures should be allied to a wider use of credit transfer. An adult whose job moves him from Aberdeen to Bristol should be able to have credit for the education he has partly completed in Scotland, and then take up the rest of the programme in his new area. To avoid such problems, and that of programmes seeming too 'à la carte' or lacking in intellectual depth, a better organization and information service would be needed throughout the United Kingdom and Northern Ireland. This already exists for the full-time degree courses at universities, polytechnics and institutes of higher education and would not seem impossible for higher education's continuing education courses.

To sum up; the adult student is beset by problems which do not affect the education of the unmarried, full-time student eighteen years old. Everything from work to family responsibilities has to be accommodated. For most continuing education students, part-time study is the only possibility. So forms of education which help such students should be developed. Two very effective aids are the use of modular course units (by which a programme can be built up from separate credits) and credit transfer, so that a move from one area to another does not mean the end of a student's course.

Proposition 3.10   There should be financial provision for a universal entitlement to continuing education.

Ours is a very unequal society. Nowhere is this inequality more apparent than in the provision of education for those over sixteen. Full-time higher education continues to be largely the preserve of the middle classes. Where paid educational leave is available it is often those who have already had the most education who receive it. This paper does not argue that such groups should now be denied the existing provision, but that it should be extended to a more numerous and broadly-based clientele. In continuing education we are in danger of developing as a service predominantly for the wealthy (who can afford it) or for the poor (who have government grants from agencies such as the MSC).

A revision of the present system of financial support is called for, so as to provide a universal entitlement to continuing education. Such proposals as a lifelong education credit system should be explored; to give each citizen the right to so much education throughout his life seems more just than the present ad hoc arrangements (see Proposition 1.2). The inevitable claim that it would be too expensive may well prove false. Many would not wish to take up their entitlement. Others would replace alternative forms of demand on the public purse by education (see Proposition 4.4). Any plea for further educational funding should also take note that we are amongst those with the lower per capita educational investments in the Western world. Even as early as 1975 Denmark, for example, spent twice as much on education per head of population as Britain did. As the years go by the gulf widens between our spending on education and that of other countries.

Proposition 3.11   Research is needed on which to base changes in continuing education.

Despite the strong research tradition of much of British higher education, continuing education has not been much examined. The reasons are legion and range from a healthy emphasis on good teaching rather than on research in university departments of adult education to the school-based research emphasis of such bodies as the DES and SSRC. There are signs of change, with leadership now coming from ACACE, DES and NIAE. On the universities' side, the creation in 1969 of the Standing Conference for University Teaching and Research in the Education of Adults encouraged an increase in research. Despite these notable improvements the cadre of researchers in continuing education remains modest and the tradition of relying only on practical experience, instead of supplementing it with research information, still dominates most areas of continuing education (see Proposition 4.3).

Decision making in continuing education needs to be firmly based on good information. Whether it be the skills needed by tutors in teaching adults, or other social costs saved by greater educational investment, or whatever, the continuing education field needs to be able to point to research findings to show the way. National initiatives such as the Russell Report of 1974 or, now, ACACE have shown the gaps which result from a too-modest research activity. Funding agencies such as the research councils, the DES, the MSC, and the private foundations should give greater priority to the field of continuing education. Professional agencies need to be bombarding such foundations with well-thought-out research proposals in this much neglected area.

Research is a powerful factor in influencing change. It is a recurrent theme of this chapter that, because of the social and economic revolution Britain is at present experiencing, life-long education is already a pressing necessity for a majority of our citizens. As is so often the case other countries have been quicker to recognize this; but practical considerations will force continuing education policies upon us. To take an obvious example, the new industries found in the Harvard-MIT Arc of Massachusetts or in Silicon Valley in California demand continuous education for their work forces.

It is characteristic of the history of English higher education that innovations tend to be introduced by the creation of new institutions, rather than by the acceptance of innovation by existing institutions. The conservative nature of Oxbridge in the 19th century ensured that new higher education needs, especially in the sciences, were met by the creation of the provincial universities. Since 1945 the polytechnics, the Council for National Academic Awards and the Open University have come into being partly because the universities would not meet new demands for technological courses, part-time first degrees and other public requirements. It is to be hoped that the fast growing new demands for continuing education receive a warmer reception from the major historic institutions of higher education.

The review of recent developments in our next section shows examples of how some of our proposals could be implemented. It also shows that in other areas much remains to be done.

EXAMPLES OF RECENT DEVELOPMENTS

This section contains examples of innovations which in the past few years have made higher education more accessible to more adults. It also notes proposals which, if implemented, could have similar effects.

The developments mentioned here are inevitably selective. One of the difficulties in encouraging the wider adoption of successful innovations is that they so often remain localized and are not always easy to find out about or to record. We do need more of this kind of information if we are to translate local successes into national practices.

Proposition 4.1   *Recent initiatives reinforce the case for wider and more flexible access.*

Most recent developments have been aimed at reducing the most important single barrier to higher education for adults: entry itself. There may be plenty of opportunities for study in Britain, but access to those opportunities can generally be difficult and daunting for most adults, not least since they often lack the initial confidence to seek to enter the higher education system. Thus the apparent availability of study opportunities should not be confused with the actual ability to gain access to them.

An outstanding example of widening access for adults is the Open College system in north-west England. This has been successful in linking Lancaster University, Preston Polytechnic and a number of further education colleges in providing students with alternative entry qualifications to school-orientated GCE 'A' levels. On the premises that the content, teaching methods and study arrangements of GCE courses are not necessarily the most appropriate form of study for most adults, no formal qualifications are needed to enter the Open College course which consists of a programme of units at Stage A (introducing basic study skills and methods and subject areas which are not formally examined) and Stage B (in a wide range of subjects formally examined through work-assessments and written examination). Stage A units generally extend over 50 hours of tuition and Stage B over 100 hours. Satisfactory completion of two Stage B units (normally preceded by four Stage A units) gives entry to Lancaster University or Preston Polytechnic.

The work of the Open College Federation is overseen by a committee reporting to the University Senate and the Polytechnic's Academic Board. Within each of the constituent colleges there is a co-ordinator responsible for administering the scheme and these co-ordinators meet regularly. The scheme has been evaluated by independent researchers who concluded that:

> '... the Open University — through the absence of formal examinations at Stage A, and by advertizing itself positively and extensively as "specially for adults" — does attract adults to return to study, many of whom would not have risked GCE courses.

It is evident that the informality, flexibility and supporting teaching of Stage A units make the Open College both an enjoyable and an educative experience for most students and enables many of them to gain a new confidence in their learning abilities, and some of them to develop an interest in higher education which had never entered their minds before.' (Percy and Lucas 1980)

The Open College has prompted a good deal of interest elsewhere, but it remains by far the most extensive of its kind in Britain. It deserves to be more widely copied: it is therefore encouraging to note a recent proposal from the Manchester LEA local education authority to set up a Manchester Open College Federation based on the higher and further education institutions in the area.

A venture in the same field, which has been more widely followed, is the 'Fresh Horizons' course initiated at the City Literary Institute's adult education centre in central London in 1966. This 'return to study' scheme has been fully documented by its original organizer, Enid Hutchinson, in *Learning Later* (1978), where she describes its novelty as 'challenging the single subject approach' as an alternative to the 'GCE route march'. Thus the original 'Fresh Horizons' curriculum package contained English language and literature, social studies, mathematics, and speech and drama, because, in Mrs Hutchinson's words: 'If they are to establish new confidence in themselves, language development is as important for adults as it is for growing children'.

These courses have appealed most strongly to women and are now available in several further education colleges, and under the extra-mural auspices of some polytechnics and universities. They have been described as a 'process of self-discovery' and have paved the way for many women to enter higher education, although students have sometimes still had to gather together 'A' level qualifications to prove their acceptability.

The acceptability and transferability of credits raises sleeping dogs which many educational administrators would prefer to allow to lie quiet. The Open University has had to make its own way here, not for entry purposes (since it is after all open to all adults over 21) but for credit exemptions in obtaining the requisite number of credits for the award of its degrees. It has equated the value of its applicants' qualifications and given appropriate credit for them. Few other higher education institutions have followed this example. But we are one step nearer to a national implementation of credit transfer arrangements through the confirmatory report of the DES's inquiry into the feasibility of such a system — the Toyne Report. The next stage of that inquiry, now in progress, should show how it might be achieved. This will free the way not just to inter-institutional co-operation, in providing courses along the lines, for example, of the link between the Open University and Bulmershe College of Higher Education and between the OU and Lancaster University, but also to inter-institutional movement by students. Part-time can be a much lengthier business than full-time study, and any substantial development of part-time study opportunities will call for recognition that students might start their studies in one institution and complete them in another. Thus, for example, and as we have already said, students whose work obliges them to move to some other part of the country or to drop their studies for a time in the middle of a course should be able to pick up where they left off rather than have to start again.

The proven ability of the Open University to accept, and to help to a successful conclusion, undergraduate students who have no prior academic qualifications (although with local provision to prepare them where necessary for degree level study) has not convinced many other institutions that they too could operate an open door policy for adult students. It is true that some do not always insist on the 'normal' qualifications for adult applicants, but this is rarely publicized beyond the small print of institutional prospectuses. The Council for National Academic Awards is therefore to be congratulated for its encouragement of more open access by mature students to its approved courses.

Institutions are of course properly anxious to maintain standards, and entry qualifications are one, but only one, way of ensuring this. Questions are now being raised about whether these qualifications for adult applicants need necessarily be exclusively academic. For some time now in the United States there has been an extensive system of assessment for 'experiential' credits to equate adults' work and life experience with educational attainment either for course entry or for academic credit purposes. This is co-ordinated by the Council for Advancement of Experiential Learning (CAEL) which currently has a membership of some 350 institutions. A recently published book by Norman Evans, *The Knowledge Revolution: Making the Link between Learning and Work* (1981) examines the American experience and suggests how it might begin to be introduced in Britain. This kind of assessment needs a good deal of organization and staff time: hence it can be fairly expensive; but intending students in the United States are apparently prepared to pay for this shortened route to higher education qualifications. As Evans says: 'Studying more carefully what you are doing day by day, and gaining a further qualification for doing so, has a common sense appeal, as well as being rooted in sound educational principles'. It remains to be seen whether this approach can cross the cultural gap between North America and Britain, but it certainly deserves consideration and we may expect to hear more of it over the next few years.

Indeed there is a sense in which we already have begun to move in this direction through independent study programmes, notably for example at North East London Polytechnic and Lancaster University. These institutions are establishing the notion that adult students can successfully negotiate with educational institutions the content of a course of study individually suited to their own needs and experience. The work at both institutions has been evaluated in *Independent Study* by Keith Percy and Paul Ramsden (1980), who conclude that '... all students should have the opportunity and experience of becoming independent learners during a part of their course of undergraduate study.'

There are of course difficulties in this form of study — not all students are suited to it, and adequate assessment can present problems — but it does provide welcome new development in widening higher education opportunities for adults. All the more regrettable therefore that the pioneering work at NELP and Lancaster, both of which began their independent study programmes in 1972, has not been more widely taken up.

However, as has been repeatedly stated here, the crucial development needed for the enlarging of continuing education in higher education is part-time study facilities — and the touchstone for any institution's commitment to this is its degree level programme. The report of the recent inquiry based at Birkbeck College (see page 42), with its catalogue of part-time degree provision in universities and polytechnics, does not make very encouraging reading (Tight 1982). In particular the universities in Britain (with the obvious exceptions of the Open University, and Birkbeck and Goldsmiths' Colleges in the University of London) offer very little. Apart from a thin scattering of part-time degrees in education, the only substantial providers — all fairly new to the field — are Hull, with seven part-time degrees, and Kent, with six. Interesting new developments are Lancaster's decision to open the first year of all undergraduate degree courses to part-time study during the day, and Stirling's decision to open all its BA and BSc general degrees to part-time study during the day over a study period of five years.

The polytechnics present a somewhat brighter picture since nearly all of them provide some part-time degree study. This is generally rather limited, but three have built up their part-time courses into double figures: Manchester 18, North-East London 11, and South Bank 10.

Malcolm Tight's report also offers some information on 'post-experience' short courses in universities and polytechnics. The data here is less precise, but it would seem that there is a great variation among institutions in the size of their provision: a few offer no provision, many provide a modest programme, and some do a great deal — notably Birmingham University with 269 courses recorded in 1979 and Central London Polytechnic which has its own Short Course Unit.

An obvious concomitant of part-time provision is distance learning. Britain has achieved international renown through the highly successful work of the Open University, but that very success seems to have led all the other institutions in higher education to keep their doors closed to distance-learning possibilities. It has been left to the independent correspondence colleges to exploit the field through the London University external degree system.

There are of course formidable difficulties in setting up distance learning facilities, not least in the capital costs of preparing the learning materials. But the further education sector has begun to move in this direction with the encouragement of development work by the Council for Educational Technology and the important contribution of the National Extension College in providing its Flexistudy materials. No doubt this will receive a further boost from the Open Tech programme when it gets underway, but it remains to be seen just what part the higher education institutions will seek to play in that programme.

The last example in this account of improvements in access to higher education is the proposal, now at the planning stage, for a 'University of the Third Age' on the 'Troisieme Age' model successfully developed in France. This is not intended to be a free-standing institution, but rather a way to make more effective use, for retired people, of available higher education resources (there are now almost 10 million retired people in Britain). The initial venture is likely to emerge in Cambridge or London in 1982. This may prove yet again to be an example of a new form of supply generating a new form of demand. If so, we can expect to see it spreading beyond Cambridge and London over the next few years.

Proposition 4.2   Recent developments give evidence of the need for local information and advisory services.

Mention of new forms of demand suggests that making access easier is not of itself going to be sufficient to induce more adults to continue their education. Many lack the confidence and the knowledge to suppose that higher or any other kind of education could be open to them. A growing awareness of this has been manifest in several recent official reports, for example the DES discussion paper *Continuing Education* and the MSC consultative document *An 'Open Tech' Programme.* Both have cited the need for more information centres which would make existing and new provision more widely known and advise enquirers about suitable opportunities. This goes beyond the inquiry desk set up within institutions at the beginning of the academic year to the idea of permanent, well-publicized, easily accessible, inter-institutional centres providing guidance on every sort of education and training need. There are currently about forty such centres in Britain, mostly operating on minimal resources, but their numbers are growing (see Advisory Council for Adult and Continuing Education 1979). Northern Ireland offers perhaps the most ambitious examples of this facility with the Northern Ireland Further Education Guidance Service and the Educational Guidance Service for Adults, both based in Belfast and both now receiving support from public educational funds.

The Open University has gained a lot of experience in this work through its admissions counselling procedures, and it is no coincidence that

CONTINUING EDUCATION 63

the OU's regional office in Leeds currently houses a British Library-financed research project to inquire into the development of educational guidance services both in public libraries and elsewhere. The Advisory Council for Adult and Continuing Education has also funded this project to find out more about the use of the present services. It is already becoming evident that many inquirers are very unclear about what they are seeking through a return to education: information and advice can be particularly helpful in clarifying this and in matching needs and aspirations to appropriate opportunities. It can also be a valuable source of information for educational institutions themselves as to the gaps in local provision. Higher education institutions can only benefit from close co-operation with these services.

Proposition 4.3   There have been some, but only a few studies of who adult students are.

Relatively little work has been done in Britain to find out about those adults who are 'volunteers for learning', and even less to discover the far greater number of adults who have never undertaken any formal education since leaving school. A few institutions, notably again the Open University, have surveyed their own enrolled students and the OU has gathered information going beyond personal characteristics to study methods and difficulties. A national study of mature students, sponsored by the DES, has recently been completed and publication can be expected in 1982. These results should help individual institutions to identify the difficulties experienced by adult students from the moment they decide to return to study, through the problems of determining what and where to study, to the actual process of following and completing a course. Those insights into actual adult students will be complemented in 1982 by the publication of the results of a national sample survey seeking to identify the adult population's educational experience and needs. Brief details of the survey, undertaken by the Advisory Council for Adult and Continuing Education, appear on pp. 42—44 (see also pp. 56—58).

Proposition 4.4   Problems of financial support for adult students are still insufficiently considered.

There is little to record in the way of recent developments so far as adult students are concerned. The present mandatory award system, remarkably generous as it is by international standards, is essentially geared to the needs of young students in 'recognized' courses of full-time study and without dependent responsibilities. It is not well adapted to the needs of adult students.

Equally, the present provision of paid educational leave (PEL), which might be thought likely to benefit all employed adults, is very distorted in its application. As a result it is young men under the age of thirty in professional and administrative posts who receive by far the greatest benefit from PEL (Killeen 1981).

Increasing concentration on part-time education, although it would not relieve the need for leave from employment, would diminish the need for specific financial support, although again it would by no means remove the need completely. It may be that the only equitable solution is the notion of an adult 'right to education', whose practical implementation would call for some form of financial credit for a specified period of education in adulthood — to be taken as and when each individual adult prefers. That has been proposed by Oliver Fulton in his chapter in the SRHE Leverhulme study *Access to Higher Education* (Fulton 1981) and is examined in more detail in the recent report by the Advisory Council for Adult and Continuing Education *Continuing Education: From Policies to Practice*. But this radical proposal is outside the scope of early action by educational institutions, which can best help at present by minimizing adult students' financial difficulties by such facilities as the payment of fees by instalments, timetabling to limit the number of journeys in attending courses, and arrangements for child care whilst parents are studying in the institution (see p.34).

Proposition 4.5 *Overall trends suggest there is growing recognition of the case for expanding continuing education.*

There is a noticeable trend both within and outside institutions towards the development of continuing education — and this is occurring despite the current adverse economic conditions. One 'non-educational' reason for this is of course the demographic shift which results in there being fewer young people in the conventional age group for education and a proportionately larger adult population. This will not manifest itself clearly in the higher education sector until the mid-1980s, but the prospect is already turning attention towards a new student clientele.

Within higher education we have the recent establishment of the Polytechnics Association for Continuing Education (PACE), while the long-established Universities Council for Adult Education has just added the word 'continuing' to its name to create UCACE. Among the professional organizations the National Association of Teachers in Further and Higher Education (NATFHE) has been actively promoting continuing education ideas with the support of its constituent body, the Association for Adult and Continuing Education (AACE). The National Association of Local Government Officers (NALGO) has recently completed a study of continuing education, both generally and within its own professional sector, and has published its report *Post-School Education*. The Trades Union Congress has been similarly active in promulgating trades union policies for continuing education. The churches have recently combined to form a Churches Association for Adult and Continuing Education (CAACE).

At central government level, too, much more interest has been shown in the education and training of adults (even if the political and funding emphasis still centres on the 16—19 age group). Hence the 1980 DES discussion paper *Continuing Education* and the more recent shift by the MSC towards the needs of adults both in its '"Open Tech" Programme' proposals and in its 'New Training Initiative' papers. The DES has also renewed the remit of the Advisory Council for Adult and Continuing Education until 1983.

So the general climate of opinion is apparently favouring the continuing education of adults. But, as has been shown here, though more attention is being given to easing access, other related problems (information and guidance, financing, etc.) are still insufficiently considered. It is possible though (and it is certainly desirable) as the decade progresses for us to look forward to extensive new developments in higher education to cater for increasing numbers of adult students.

CONCLUSION

The case made in the preceding pages is strong: to open doors, to be ready to make major changes in attitudes and so in the style of institutions, to compensate more for the initially disadvantaged, to get away from the 'front end' view of education, to create more inter-institutional co-operation, to be in all things more flexible. The case is both economic and moral.

There are many inhibitions at present, notably in the educational regulations themselves. But regulations reflect dominant attitudes. As they change, so will the regulations about such things as qualifications, 'credit transfer', and all the rest. The potential demand is greater than all but a few realize. As it is tapped, so the pressure for changes in the educational system as a whole will grow.

At the end of this process, looking to many at present like a pipe-dream, is the idea of a *right* to continuing education and so to consequent financial provision. As the eighties pass it is likely to seem less and less of a wild idea. The decline in the number of eighteen-year-olds will accelerate its acceptance. But the strongest test of one's commitment to the idea of more continuing education lies in whether one can answer 'yes' to the following question: If no more money in total were available for education as a whole, would you be willing to accept a redistribution of resources: one which, say, gave relatively less to 18—21-year-olds so that older and part-time students could have better access and provision?

REFERENCES

Advisory Council for Adult & Continuing Education (ACACE) (1979) *Links to Learning* Leicester: ACACE

Advisory Council for Adult & Continuing Education (ACACE) (1982) *Adults: Their Educational Experience and Needs* Chap.VI: Current participation in adult & continuing education. Leicester: ACACE

Advisory Council for Adult & Continuing Education (ACACE) (1982) *Continuing Education: From Policies to Practice* Leicester: ACACE

Department of Education & Science (DES) (1980) *Continuing Education. Post Experience Vocational Provision for those in Employment: A paper for discussion* London: DES

Evans, N. (1981) *The Knowledge Revolution: Making the Link between Learning and Work* London: Grant McIntyre Ltd

Fulton, O. (Editor) (1981) *Access to Higher Education* Leverhulme Programme of Study into the Future of Higher Education, Volume 2. Guildford: Society for Research into Higher Education

Hutchinson, Enid (1978) *Learning Later* London: Routledge & Kegan Paul

Hutchison, E. (1963) Adult education. In Peterson, A.D.C. (Editor) *Techniques of Teaching* Volume 3. Oxford: Pergamon

Killeen, J. and Bird, Margaret (1981) *Education and Work* Leicester: National Institute of Adult Education (NIAE)

Lilley, S. (1980) *Discovering Relativity for Yourself* Cambridge: Cambridge University Press

Manpower Services Commission (MSC) (1981 — 82) *New Training Initiative* (papers): 1) *A Consultative Document* May 1981; 2) *An Agenda for Action* December 1981; 3) *Youth Task Group Report* April 1982. London: MSC

Manpower Services Commission (MSC) (1981) *An Open Tech Programme* (consultative document) London: MSC

Marriot, S. (1981) *A Backstairs to a Degree: Studies in Adult and Continuing Education* University of Leeds: Department of Adult Educational and Extra-mural Studies

Percy, K. and Lucas, S.M. (Editors) (1980) *The Open College and Alternatives* University of Lancaster

Percy, K. and Ramsden, P. (1980) *Independent Study* Guildford: Society for Research into Higher Education

Tight, M. (1982) *Part-time Degree Level Study in the United Kingdom* Leicester: Advisory Council for Adult and Continuing Education (ACACE)

Toyne, P. (1979) *Educational Credit Transfer: Feasibility Study; final report* Funded by the Department of Education and Science

Roderick, G.W. (1981) *Mature Students in Further and Higher Education* University of Sheffield

Wagner, L., Fulton, O., Percy, K. and Woodley, A. (1982) *Mature Student Participation in Education* (Central London Polytechnic/ Lancaster University/Open University joint project sponsored by the DES. To be published early 1983.)

Woodhall, Maureen (1980) *The Scope and Costs of the Education and Training of Adults in Britain* Study commissioned by Advisory Council for Adult and Continuing Education (ACACE). Leicester: ACACE

3

THE CURRICULUM OF HIGHER EDUCATION

by Sinclair Goodlad and Brian Pippard with Donald Bligh

SUMMARY
This chapter offers some suggestions about ways of thinking about the curriculum in higher education and considers possible policies to provide for flexibility and innovation. Although there are important differences of orientation and tradition between universities, polytechnics, and institutes of higher education, the chapter makes no systematic distinction between them, but rather concentrates on institutional issues relevant to all sectors of higher education.

To facilitate discussion in the seminar, the argument is articulated around the following sixteen propositions.

1.0 PROFESSIONALISM AND A SENSE OF PURPOSE
1.1 Curricula in higher education should involve an appropriate balance between theory and practice and should take into account the needs of society and of the individual learner.
1.2 Curricula in higher education should demonstrate structure in thought and should lead students to the experience of 'authoritative uncertainty'.
1.3 The curriculum objectives of individual students' courses should be balanced, as well as those of the total provision made by an institution and by the educational system as a whole.
2.0 ACTIVITY FOR LEARNING
2.1 Curricula in higher education should where possible and appropriate encourage in students an action-oriented, operational style of thinking.
2.2 Curricula in higher education should where possible involve periods of practical activity intercalated with periods of academic reflection with work designed both to achieve specific integration between the two and to demonstrate the learning which has taken place so that this may be credited in the award of the degree.
2.3 In commuter universities, where informal contact between staff and students may be difficult to achieve, opportunities should be provided for undergraduates to assist with staff members' research.
2.4 A feasibility study should be carried out concerning the possibility of action agencies having education officers on their staff, paid for if necessary from DES funds, whose tasks would be to draw students into the agencies for the practical part of their studies and

to arrange interchange of senior personnel.
3.0 FLEXIBLE PATTERNS OF GENERAL AND SPECIALIST COURSES
3.1 Entry into higher education should be made less dependent on examination success in specialist subjects.

3.2 At each critical point in the educational system, the nature and content of courses should be primarily determined by the needs of those who are leaving education at that point.

3.3 Existing 3-year specialized university courses should be replaced by 2-year general courses. Student grants should be available very widely for these two years, but the numbers supported on advanced courses might be broadly influenced by the need for specialists. Such a radical change cannot be carried through without extensive preliminary work.

3.4 Each year of each student's curriculum should provide for a student's own project.

4.0 PROFESSIONAL STANDARDS AND ASSESSMENT
4.1 Assessment in higher education should reflect a conception of academic excellence as involving the ability to think to some purpose.

4.2 Whenever possible, higher education institutions should state what is to be assessed rather than how and when students are to learn.

4.3 Professional institutions and the CNAA should offer to assess anyone prepared to pay the assessment fees and should not also require attendance at specific courses.

5.0 TOWARDS PROFESSIONAL FLEXIBILITY
5.1 Procedures should be examined, both at system and at institution level, to secure the possibility of curriculum innovation.

5.2 Research is needed into several areas which vitally affect curricula.

INTRODUCTION

A curriculum is a regular course of study or training at a school or university (OED). In so far as form and content can be distinguished, the curriculum refers primarily to the *content* of education; more particularly to that which students are *required* to study. Curricula are, therefore, political; they represent compromises between what is individually desirable (such as unfettered intellectual inquiry) and what is institutionally possible. Today it is more than ever necessary to stimulate discussion about possible principles of good practice, not least because the sheer size of the higher education system in the United Kingdom invites public scrutiny of efficiency. The claims of academics for special treatment (tenure) and for the privilege of academic freedom are beginning to be objects of ridicule. Perhaps in a small-scale and inexpensive higher education system academics could afford not to justify their procedures; but in a large system, funded from the public purse, they must.

We believe that institutions of higher education should move towards recognition that their social function is the primary one, but that it cannot be carried out without the presence of the highest possible standards (a) at every level of teaching, in the dedication of teachers and in their technical accomplishment, (b) in pushing learning to the limits of knowledge for a few (whose needs must not distort the pattern for the rest), and (c) in providing opportunities for research for the gifted.

All this demands changes of attitude which must spring from within institutions of higher education; therefore the structure must positively encourage the initiative of individual innovators and do so within a severely limited budget. We are aware that there have been many distinguished attempts to formulate a systematic rationale for curricula in higher education — for example, the famous Harvard 'Red Book' *General Education in a Free Society* (1945), Daniel Bell's *The Reforming of General Education* (1966), Huston Smith's *The Purposes of Higher Education* (1955), and, more recently, Boyer and Levine's *A Quest for Common Learning* (1981) and the Carnegie Commission report *Content and Context* (Kaysen 1973). Other works have examined the role of particular types of subjects — for example, the humanities (Niblett 1974, 1975) or engineering (Finniston 1980). We are aware too of many experiments with curricula in the last twenty years — for example in new universities (cf Daiches 1964) and in polytechnics and institutes of higher education (cf CNAA *Directory of First Degree Courses*) and of radical experiments such as the schools of independent studies at Lancaster University and the North East London Polytechnic (cf Percy and Ramsden 1980). We have not, however, written a survey of current practice, nor an analytical review of research. Our brief was to write a reasoned policy statement and our aim has, therefore, been to suggest some ideas which might lead to a loosening up of the system so that different institutions might follow different paths and initiate experiments which others might care to adopt. We have also concentrated on those matters into which our personal experience has given us insight.

Before listing the specific propositions around which our discussion is arranged, we wish to stress the following points. First, this chapter is not a systematic exegesis of curriculum based upon a unified system of philosophical, psychological, sociological, or historical theory; rather it is an attempt to deal pragmatically with some important curriculum issues. We hope, however, that our views are both internally consistent and philosophically defensible, and that they are based upon a reading of individual and social psychology and an analysis of institutional possibility which, while representing no dramatic break with tradition (the organic and complex network of arrangements by which higher education has taken its present form), is nevertheless sufficiently radical to point the way towards rapid change where this is needed.

Secondly, the curriculum of higher education could in principle cover any or all areas of human knowledge; we cannot possibly pronounce judgement on any but the curricula with which we are familiar. To attempt to do so might suggest, contrary to our intention, that we want to set limits to human learning. We are vividly aware that learning goes on elsewhere than in institutions specifically devoted to higher education and not just in a person's late teens and early twenties. It is a matter of great interest and importance to decide what are the best conditions for different kinds of learning. To suggest points of administrative and institutional continuity we have sketched some salient features of existing academic disciplines. In addition, we have examined the use of intercalated periods of academic reflection and practical activity (sandwich placements, internships, study service, and so on) which involve learning outside formal academic environments.

Thirdly, we wish to remain faithful to the perception that higher education is not only a means to some other end (such as employment) but also an end in itself. Use must be balanced by delight. The old adage that one works to live, and does not just live to work, reminds us that whatever else it does higher education must simultaneously fire the imagination, challenge the intellect, excite moral consciousness, and, in short, provide direct encounters with the ideas and artefacts which are the finest products of civilization. Although much of what we say below concerns education for the professions, and the need to encourage throughout higher education more operational, purposeful styles of thinking than have been universally familiar, we believe, and hope that we demonstrate, that thinking to some purpose is not incompatible with free-ranging intellectual enquiry.

Fourthly, we take it for granted that higher education should be a privilege open to as many people as possible. The unattainable ideal would be for every citizen to have the chance to learn as much about the body and about health as a doctor, as much about physical systems as an engineer, as much about poetry as a professor of literature, and so on. We would like to see education organized to produce the fewest possible restrictions on the opportunity of everyone to learn everything. Pragmatically, this involves trying to use the opportunities of the curriculum to cause everyone to want to know more, providing as much freedom as possible for the (perhaps anomalous) highly curious and energetic student, while recognizing that less able students may need firm guidelines. We have, therefore, devoted some space to discussion of institutional structures with a view to discerning those structures which would optimize opportunities for learning within the limits of available funding.

Fifthly, much higher education is (and has been since universities grew originally around the professions of law, medicine, and divinity), concerned with preparation for work. Even subjects apparently remote from contexts of immediate utility often have more than vestigial relevance to occupations outside higher education and almost all involve a 'hidden curriculum' of styles of thinking and skills of wide general application. We have, therefore, devoted space to the use of problem solving as a method of encouraging a more organized and structured process of thinking than may at present be practised in some higher education curricula.

Finally, although we recognize that there are important differences of orientation and tradition between universities, polytechnics, and institutes of higher education, we have made no systematic distinction in our writing between the different types of institution. Not only would it be tedious continually to be drawing fine distinctions between the different types of institution, but also our concern is to address structural issues relevant to all sectors of higher education. For example, individual departments in universities may be as 'applied' as any in polytechnics; individual departments in polytechnics or institutes of education may be as 'pure' as any in universities. Likewise, the traditional association of teaching and research demanded of lecturers in universities is but one manifestation of what we regard as essential for any teacher at any level of education: continuous engagement in some form or other (practice, consultancy, manufacture, creation, criticism, as well as research and scholarship of the more conventional kind) with those aspects of the teacher's subject that represent either intellectual innovation or application outside institutions of higher education or both.

PROFESSIONALISM AND A SENSE OF PURPOSE

Proposition 1.1
Curricula in higher education should involve an appropriate balance between theory and practice and should take into account the needs of society and of the individual learner.

Unless institutions of higher education are to try to be all things to all men (and thus to lose all institutional coherence and amour propre), they must have a principle of selection in what they do. All social institutions have an educative function (churches, factories, sporting clubs, and family) if only to school members in the requirements of social roles; similarly, learning goes on anywhere and everywhere. It is, therefore, useful to have a model to provide a framework for understanding the differences from, and similarities to, other forms of education or curricula in higher education. We have found that the following ideas provide a convenient conceptual map to place existing higher education curricular in context.

```
                    Theory
                      |
      Society ————————+———————— Individual
                      |
                   Practice
```

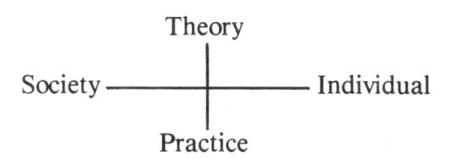

Theory: A complex of ideas internally consistent and rich in interconnections with other areas of inquiry.
Practice: Some connection, however remote, with practical questions of how to survive and why to survive
Society: A rationale justifying the subject or discipline's place in the affairs of society and its claim to a share of public money and to the time and attention of talented people
Individual: The capacity to nourish each student's sense of identity, and competence and meaning

---

The divisions between these concepts are artificial and are made for heuristic purposes only. For example, the 'Individual' is dependent upon 'Society' for identity (being in one important sense an aggregation of roles) just as the concept of 'Society' is meaningless until individuals or groups are specified. Similarly, 'Theory' is valueless without 'Practice' and all practice implies theory. (To adapt Sartre: not to have a theory is itself a theory.) The value of separating out these concepts, which inform many effective curricula in contemporary higher education, is that they emphasize the differences between higher learning in its *institutional* forms and similar learning as practised by *individuals.* Compare, for example, a radio 'ham' with an electrical engineer, an antiquary with an historian, a naturalist with a botanist, a journalist with a political scientist. In each of the first listings in the pairs, the practitioner operates without reference to one or other of the institutional criteria by which we find it useful to describe existing higher education.

The emphasis on Theory distinguishes academic studies from their culturally primary correlates: eg cooking/nutrition; construction/engineering; worship/theology; literature/literary criticism; politics/political science; musical performance/musicology. The primary form is just as useful (often, in fact, more useful in some senses) than its manifestation in higher education. The point of the distinctions is to urge that institutional coherence comes from a certain concentration of effort. Institutions of higher education have become good at explanations, classifications, analysis; other types of institution are better at developing the primary cultural forms (eg restaurants, factories, churches, theatres, parliament, conservatoires). For depth of understanding in any field of learning, it may, as we argue below, be necessary for a student of nutrition both to study biochemistry and to work in a kitchen, for an engineer both to study strength of materials and economics and to work on a production line, for a theology student both to study biblical criticism and to work in church or mission agency, for a student of literature both to study literary criticism and to work in a publishing house or a theatre, for a political science student both to study political theory and to work as research assistant to a national or local politician, for a music student both to study musicology and to play an instrument, etc....

The emphasis on Practice prevents study drifting off into meaninglessness or crankiness. Practice alone is, of course, not enough; without some co-ordinating theory, some systematic inter-connectedness of ideas or programme of study for the future, purely practical subjects can ossify or degenerate into a congeries of rules of thumb and itsy-bitsy obsession with technique. It can also be extraordinarily conservative in every sense including the political. But without some attempt to demonstrate the application of ideas academic theory can become arcane, unintelligible, self-congratulatory, or simply trivial.

The emphasis on Society recalls that academic disciplines are *institutional* phenomena, with all the paraphernalia of learned societies, journals, peer assessment, and such like. Some types of innovative thinker can, and perhaps should, work outside academic institutions (as did the French philosophers) until the locating of an intellectual concern within a public tradition can generate public funding. Precisely how this element of social accountability is to be worked out in any individual case may be difficult to say; we express concern below (p. 80) about the growing, and even perhaps excessive influence of professional and paraprofessional validating bodies on the form and content of higher education curricula. Suffice it to say at this point that curricula in higher education should have an explicit social rationale.

The emphasis on the Individual helps to force attention onto the fundamental purpose of study for each individual student. Totalitarian systems, of whatever political complexion, treat individuals not as ends in themselves but as means to some other end. By contrast, education in liberal democracies must preserve and nourish the perception of the individual in higher education, even though, to be professionally competent, he or she must submit to a severe discipline. While the notion of studying a subject 'for its own sake' may cut little ice, it is nevertheless important to give free play to the individual student's imagination. Many students will be happy to be firmly guided; but no curriculum in higher education should leave out the self-motivated student's opportunity to follow ideas wherever they may lead. Scholarship may be an essential ingredient in higher education, but it is not its raison d'etre: however disagreeable the notion may be to academics, scholarship is a by-product except for the very few.

Proposition 1.2
Curricula in higher education should demonstrate structure in thought and should lead students to the experience of 'authoritative uncertainty'.

One aim of every different degree curriculum should be to give each student the experience of 'authoritative uncertainty' — the perception of what still needs to be found out in a given field based upon depth of understanding of what is already known.

As we have argued above (Proposition 1.1), all social institutions have an educative function, and many social institutions (such as newspapers and radio and television companies) disseminate knowledge. What distinguishes higher education institutionally is that the knowledge it deals in is highly structured according to principles which can be systematically expounded. Teachers in higher education may not know more than (they may even know less than) the individual practitioner; the radio 'ham' may have more raw information than an electrical engineer, the antiquary more specific facts than the historian, and so on. Teachers in higher education exhibit 'authoritative uncertainty' when they know, on the basis of highly organized study, what is worth trying to find out and why. Their uncertainty is not that of sheer ignorance, but rather the uncertainty of deep learning. If it is this experience of 'authoritative uncertainty' that gives intellectual identity to teachers in higher education, it follows that it is this that they should most vigorously try to convey to their students (cf Goodlad 1976).

The only valid intellectual role model for the teacher in higher education to offer is himself/herself; to do otherwise is to exhibit bad faith and to run the risk of inauthenticity. This does not preclude the voluntary acceptance and transmission of the ideas of others which may aid understanding. Nor does it involve teachers offering their complete personalities as models. Part of what is to be taught is obviously mastery — which in turn involves the sheer satisfaction of competence in a style of thinking or a skill. But it is the application of skill and thought to new conditions, new problems, that is the distinctive component of practice at the highest levels of all intellectual endeavour, where mastery is not enough, where one has gone beyond the pre-existing structures of thought and has to make sense of data by oneself.

Within a discipline there are uncertainties which can be resolved without changing the structure of the discipline (eg Is the proton a stable particle?). Then there is the uncertainty which (cf Kuhn 1970) involves a paradigm change (eg the wave/particle duality). The experience of these types of uncertainty can probably best be generated by intensive study of one topic within a specialist field. Often, however, the pressure of communicating established ideas eliminates discussion even of the first of these types of uncertainty. If space or opportunity can be made for extreme uncertainty, so much the better.

One useful form of the experience of uncertainty can be generated by the application of ideas to new conditions where the student has the opportunity to make a personal synthesis of ideas. What is important is for the student to experience the excitement and delight of trying to make sense of data by constructing concepts and hypotheses — even if these turn out to be 'wrong' when viewed from the vantage point of wider information. It follows that to try to 'cover the ground' or 'survey the field' is an academic objective of uncertain merit. Certainly it may be necessary for a student to be examined on a wide range of information; it does not follow that the precious (ie both expensive and desirable) moments of encounter between teacher and learner should be dissipated in 'teaching' (offering direct instruction) in topics which can be learned by the students by themselves. Collaborative work in problem solving or in research (where the student assists the staff member — see Proposition 6 below) may be one important, and often neglected, potential area of curriculum.

A short cut to the experience of uncertainty (although not quite of 'authoritative' uncertainty) can be achieved by 'cultural migration', seeing the apparent certainties in one discipline from the perspective of another discipline and thereby, perhaps, understanding the limited context in which they are certainties. To this end, for example, physics could be inspected from the perspective of philosophy, literature from anthropology, engineering from economics, philosophy from sociology, anthropology from history, etc.... The 'disturbing' perspective will vary from discipline to discipline. What is involved in each case, however, is an attempt to stimulate awareness of the strengths and weaknesses of specific intellectual positions. If graduates are to value the contribution higher education makes to their thinking, they must somehow be given, through their curricula, both the confidence which arises from mastery and the humility and tolerance (perhaps one of the major contributions of higher education to democratic and pluralist thought) which comes from the tentativeness which is experienced at the limits of competence. Curricula which neglect this element of study may produce arrogant and insensitive graduates.

Our argument for arranging the curriculum to offer students this experience of 'authoritative uncertainty' has been offered in institutional terms — the aim being to let students experience at first hand the intellectual, and associated emotional, excitement and disturbance which animates their teachers and which is the fundamental raison d'etre of their colleges. Strong support for this orientation appears in the writings of William G. Perry (1970, 1981) whose concepts of cognitive and ethical growth are commanding increasing attention as a possible psychological model to inform curriculum development in higher education.

Proposition 1.3.
The curriculum objectives of individual students' courses should be balanced, as well as those of the total provision made by an institution and by the educational system as a whole.

Certain subjects are better than others at offering the respective concentration of attention on Theory, Practice, Society, and the Individual. For example, mathematical modelling in various disciplines demonstrates the great organizing power of concepts, and, thus, the co-ordinating, economical, and potent effect of Theory. Economics and sociology often make direct study of social needs and of the claims of various interest groups; it is not difficult in these disciplines to be aware of the social accountability of education. Similarly, literature, history, philosophy, the traditional humanities subjects, powerfully nourish individual sensibility. The practical, craft element of much engineering gives direct experience of Practice and the delight and satisfaction of making and doing. It is certainly necessary to have a balance of objectives at system level in higher education: the University Grants Committee, for example, must have a responsibility for seeing that, in the university sector of the higher education system at least, the needs of the country for theory and practice and for disciplines which foster individual sensibility are met within the constraints of finance.

It may also be desirable, even necessary, that individual institutions (universities, polytechnics, institutes of higher education) have a balance of objectives represented within their curriculum offerings and, therefore, within their faculties. It does not, of course, follow that they need try to achieve a complete spread in their research because staff who teach at one institution can (and often do) readily undertake research in other institutions. Our concern is, however, to urge that the balance of objectives we have adumbrated have meaning in terms of the studies undertaken by individual students (as well as at system or institution level) so that each individual student experiences these dimensions of education if not within each activity (lecture course, project, seminar, etc.) then at least within the degree course as a whole. To fail to seek such a balance for each individual student is to risk treating students as means rather than as ends, as parts of a larger entity rather than as microcosms of mankind.

It has long been the practice in technological institutions to try to achieve something of the balance we recommend by processes of 'lateral enrichment', the addition to technical studies (which run the risk of overemphasizing the purely Practical) of compensatory chunks of other disciplines — from the humanities, offering the opportunity for Individual reflection, and/or from the social sciences (particularly economics and industrial sociology), offering the opportunity to locate technique within its appropriate industrial context. Frequently, however, such activities have had a chequered fate. For example, they are often taught by visiting lecturers from service departments who may know relatively little about the main disciplines of the students whom they teach and who have little opportunity for informal contact with either staff or students in the departments which they visit. Sometimes the students see the 'liberal studies' as unwelcome appendages to the mainstream studies. Typically, however, 'liberal studies' of this sort have failed because there is no point of convergence with the technical studies. Even when experiments have been made, for example, in sponsoring socio-technical projects in engineering education (cf Goodlad 1977), it has been difficult to keep up the momentum partly because an institutional ethos of conventionally taught courses (of lectures, tutorials/laboratories, and unseen three-hour examinations) militates against studies which throw the responsibility for synthesis onto students, but also because lecturers seeking the international visibility through publication which will ensure survival if not promotion are loathe to meddle with issues outside their immediate concerns.

Some of the most effective linkages between Theory and Practice, Social accountability and Individual intellectual stimulation, have taken place in projects involving students in activity of direct practical social utility within the context of their studies (cf. Brown and Goodlad 1974). Two elements of this work merit further attention: the problem-solving element (discussed in Proposition 4 below) and the element of interwoven academic reflection and practical activity (discussed in Proposition 5 below).

ACTIVITY FOR LEARNING

Proposition 2.1
Curricula in higher education should where possible and appropriate encourage in students an action-oriented, operational style of thinking.

It is a paradox that higher education is usually structured around disciplines, which are themselves often based on 'forms of knowledge' (Hirst 1974), whereas the practical problems upon which graduates will be employed fall at best into 'fields', requiring input from several disciplines — interdisciplinarity. Or at worst they do not fit with the preoccupations of *any* existing disciplines and require, therefore, a transdisciplinary approach (CERI 1972; Nuffield Foundation GRIHE 1975). Although (for reasons explored at length by Nisbet (1971)) we do not think that institutions of higher education should be organized around specific practical problems, we nevertheless believe (following Birch 1981) that there is a strong case for much higher education to encourage in students an operational style of thinking based upon high-level problem solving, where boundaries between disciplines must be set aside.

We believe that certain external pressures upon higher education indicate the need for some change of orientation. It is always extremely difficult to determine whether or not views which receive publicity are or are not representative of opinions held widely; however, the list of external factors given below (derived from a paper given to the OECD by William Birch in October 1981) accords largely with our own views. We therefore argue as follows.

First, the opening of higher education to a relatively wide section of the population following the recommendations of the Robbins committee has had important political consequences. Not only has it increased the public visibility of the high cost of providing higher education, but it has sharpened the public's expectations that higher education will contribute to the social and economic well-being of the country. Graduates also expect that their studies will improve their employment prospects. These factors add up to a pressure for 'relevance'.

Secondly, in a period of economic decline and financial retrenchment, when many public needs are competing for scarce resources, it is inevitable that questions should be asked as to the appropriateness of considerable public expenditure on degree courses which do not appear to equip students to make a significant contribution to the evident needs of the country.

Thirdly, the rapid progress of technological change and the increasing complexity of contemporary society (and the problems to which this complexity gives rise) have brought into question the ability of graduates to address themselves to significant issues without a more direct preparation for professional life. Educationally, the argument for dealing with vocational preparation at the postgraduate stage remains attractive. However, in a period of scarce resources and high unemployment it becomes more difficult to sustain.

Fourthly, industry, commerce, and the public services in the United Kingdom have traditionally placed great reliance upon recruiting potential top managers and administrators from graduates with high honours in the arts. This practice assumes that such students will have acquired both the intellectual training and the quality of mind to learn through experience and to exercise sound judgement in professional work. Not surprisingly, questions have been raised about the need for a stronger recruitment of scientists and technologists who arguably might be expected to have more fully developed analytical skills in, and a more ready grasp of, technological questions than arts graduates, and thus a sounder basis for exercising judgement over a wide range of contemporary issues.

Fifthly, the range of 'learned professions' has increased greatly as the fabric of society has become more administratively elaborate and more advanced technologically. A variety of bodies have promoted degree-level studies leading to professional recognition in such fields as design, surveying and estate management, accountancy, construction, environmental health, urban and regional planning, and teacher education.

There are of course many other pressures upon higher education, and, indeed, pressures operating in directions opposed to those we (following

Birch) have listed. The pressures described above do, however, demand some sort of response.

First, we do not believe that all, or indeed even most, higher education should attempt to be 'relevant' in the sense of offering direct preparation for work. Many degree courses, however, are contextually relevant to a wide range of occupations; all that is required is that this contextual relevance be more vigorously emphasized. Where studies have complex cultural objectives (such as extending our understanding of the infinite mystery and variety of human institutions, artefacts, and ideas), what may be needed is a determined and lucid statement of their claim for attention (cf. Minogue 1973). This might deter students whose aims are narrowly vocational; but that in turn might be a consummation devoutly to be wished.

Secondly, the second, third, and fourth pressures on higher education which we list above (those emphasizing the increased range and complexity of technological problems facing graduates) suggest that many degree courses would benefit by having elements (project work, sandwich placements, etc. — see below) which give specific opportunity for students to experience the world of work and to draw upon the theoretical insights of academic disciplines in attempting to formulate solutions to practical problems.

Thirdly, we are anxious that validating bodies in nascent or recently-degree-conscious professions should share our interest in ensuring that each student's studies recognize the claims of the Individual as well as of Society, of Theory as well as of Practice (see Proposition 1.1 above). If a transdisciplinary discipline were to be worked out with care and in detail, there might be little danger that any one of these considerations be neglected. But we suspect (and, in some cases from our own observation, know) that many professional courses are in fact stitched together from bits and pieces of existing (and thus respectable?) disciplines with, perhaps, less than adequate fidelity either to the needs of the profession or to those of the student.

One way in which we believe a suitable shift in orientation to many studies could take place is by the encouraging in students of more action-oriented, operational styles of thinking, through high-level problem solving.

Lest we be thought to be trivializing degree studies by what we are proposing, we might first distinguish high-level problem solving from exercises which may involve the solving of problems. The 'problems' at the end of the chapter of a textbook enable students to practise the application of certain principles guaranteed to produce certain results; there may even be published 'correct' answers. This type of problem solving helps students to extend their repertoire of techniques. By contrast, high-level problem solving requires study of questions to which there can be no guarantee that there is an 'answer', let alone a 'right' answer. High-level problem solving commonly requires the synthesis of ideas from a variety of disciplines and ultimately a judgement (political, philosophical, aesthetic, historical, moral) which requires one to think, and argue, back to first principles and indeed to the ultimate uncertainites at the centre of disciplines — in short, to the point of authoritative uncertainty where what is not known, nor even knowable, is even more important than that which is known.

It might at first sight seem self-evident that high-level problem solving is the raison d'etre of certain technological professions and, for that reason, the core of professional studies. But a remarkable number, for example, of engineering studies dissolve into a congeries of short lecture courses which break interesting problems down into smaller (and, perhaps, therefore uninteresting?) ones ('Optimize X with respect to Y', 'List the properties of...', etc.) without ever (or perhaps not until a student's final year — when enthusiasm has flagged) engaging the student with the full complexity — social, political, economic, as well as technical — of a real engineering problem. Similarly, in medicine, the McMaster medical education scheme, which is based upon problem solving (cf Barrows and Tamblyn 1980) is still regarded as somewhat revolutionary.

Most academics are vividly aware that their disciplines progress primarily through high-level problem solving. One has only to read the minutes of a faculty board in English or in sociology (or most other arts or social science disciplines) to see that very broad or fuzzy proposals for PhD research are universally resisted in favour of very specific studies. This is not because faculties of English are not interested in the meaning of life or faculties of sociology in the distribution of power in society; in the last analysis those are the questions which sustain the disciplines. Rather, general treatises are resisted because often they lack a cutting edge or focus; more precise 'problem solving' provides an opportunity for the PhD student to relate the major preoccupations of a discipline to the articulation of a representative question, to focus techniques in the interests of clarifying specific issues, and so on.

Similarly, at undergraduate level in the humanities and social sciences in particular, students' work is often based upon essay writing which in turn often involves the assaying or testing of propositions. It is no accident that arts graduates are recruited to the civil service and policy-forming branches of industry; the skills of organizing complex thoughts and large quantities of data in the defence or refutation of propositions is a 'problem-solving' skill much needed in administration. What is, perhaps, needed at both post-graduate and undergraduate level is a more self-conscious and systematic celebration of these dimensions of study, a deliberate unveiling of these elements of the 'hidden curriculum'. Often, graduates who intuitively perceive that their learning is as much about process as about product have no difficulty in switching fields or of moving serenely from academic work to admistration in commerce or public affairs. What is tragic is that many graduates feel that their education is in some important sense 'wasted' if they cannot continue to exercise their minds on arcane matters. We are convinced that a more operational style of thinking (based upon problem solving) is not incompatible with the cultivation of individual sensibility, delight, moral awareness, etc., or with engagement at the highest level with theory (independent, inter-linked networks of concepts which have an intellectual fascination and explanatory power far beyond anything needed for solving specific problems). Indeed, encounter with Theory (explanatory concepts) would seem to us to be more attractive *after* students have encountered the problems which the concepts help to illuminate.

Many of the most interesting problems occur in everyday situations. The interest is because not only do the practical questions eliminate the artificial distinctions between Theory and Practice which institutional arrangements (such as lectures and laboratory classes) may artificially emphasize, but also because most problems only emerge because of changing social conditions/needs/expectations. Examples can be drawn not only from technology or other action subjects (traffic control; care of the elderly; long-term effects of drugs, food additives, etc.; interference-free information transmission; etc.) but also from the humanities as their preoccupations are embodied in practical affairs (maintaining live theatre with increasing costs; publishing poetry or serious fiction in a market dominated by 'blockbusters'; selecting artefacts for exhibition in museums which are overflowing with material; selecting which historical records to preserve; philosophical justifications of treatment of prisoners, pre-frontal leuchotomy, vivisection, abortion, compensatory education, etc.). The modest disruption of existing syllabi to accommodate a more problem-oriented approach would do no violence to the raison d'etre of most disciplines and might generate a sense of purpose in many students.

Proposition 2.2
Curricula in higher education should where possible involve periods of practical activity intercalated with periods of academic reflection with work designed both to achieve specific integration between the two and to demonstrate the learning which has taken place so that this may be credited in the award of the degree.

If students' education is to involve a suitable balance between Theory and Practice, Social and Individual concerns, and if it is to encourage an operational style of thinking which arises from problem-solving work at a high level of conceptual density, it will be necessary to give students direct, practical experience of action agencies in which they encounter a multiplicity of problems to which their thinking can be devoted. This style of work already has a long and distinguished history in such fields as engineering (through sandwich courses), medicine (through clinical studies), law (through articles and through 'clinical' studies — cf Zander 1974), social work (through placements), and teaching (through supervised teaching practice).

In the United States experiential learning thrives in many disciplines outside the immediately recognizable professions. For example, history students help in museums, science students may be involved in pollution monitoring, sociology students in community action agencies, and so on. Already there is abundant literature describing such work (cf Duley 1981; Chickering 1977).

There is sometimes a danger that the practical experience will not be integrated into the student's academic reflection (cf Smithers 1976). But experience is growing in the systematic evaluation and academic assessment (grading) of work undertaken outside the immediate control of academic staff. For example, the Council for the Advancement of Experiential Learning (CAEL) in the United States has produced abundant handbooks and manuals for the sensitizing of students to the opportunities of learning from practical experience and for the retrospective analysis of experience gained (cf Willingham 1977). The obvious need is for curricula to have elements (essays, reports, dissertations, seminars) which systematically encourage students to integrate their placement learning and their academic learning: this cannot be left to chance.

One difficulty likely to be encountered in the early years of such work is that students' experiences inevitably differ both in the intellectual and emotional demands put upon them and in the ease or difficulty of organizing one's thoughts about the fieldwork experiences. (Problem definition is often more difficult than problem solving!) One expedient extensively used in the United States (for example by the University of Maryland) is to interlock two courses: a straight academic course (which can be validly and reliably graded in the conventional manner and which may be largely theoretical) and an experiential course (where the students' various types of academic product are graded on a pass-fail basis with the agency supervisor's report being taken into account). The condition of being awarded the grade on the academic (theoretical) course is to have achieved a pass on the experiential (practical) course.

The minimum effect of experiential learning is to offer students the opportunity to stand back from routine academic work to reflect on how their academic discipline holds together, what its outcomes are in employment, and most fundamentally what it all means to the students in a personal sense. One technique available in practically any discipline is that of tutoring, in which students can help with the teaching of other students, or more probably school pupils, less well informed than themselves (cf Goodlad 1979). For example, students from Imperial College help with the teaching of science, mathematics, and engineering in five inner London schools on Wednesday afternoons. Some students value the activity for offering them the chance to see what teaching looks like at close quarters; some have subsequently decided to enter the profession, while others have decided, before commiting a year to a PGCE, that they would be happier in some other occupation. Most students value the practice they get in the simple communication of scientific ideas (a skill important in most science-based professions), and the chance to meet people with social backgrounds different from their own.

Proposition 2.3
In commuter universities, where informal contact between staff and students may be difficult to achieve, opportunities should be provided for undergraduates to assist with staff members' research.

Our ideal form of higher education involves a seamless web of curriculum-controlled learning and learning generated by private passions and enthusiasm. Osmotic learning, by informal contact between staff and students, may, however, be difficult to achieve in 9-to-5 commuter universities. Accordingly, we commend to attention another form of experiential learning relatively easy to organize, that of undergraduate research opportunities. At Massachusetts Institute of Technology (MIT) undergraduates have the opportunity to collaborate with members of staff in staff members' research work (cf MacVicar 1976). (The word 'research' is taken to embrace traditional research and scholarship and also consultancy — indeed all of a staff member's professional work.) Work is fitted into the times left free from the students' regular classes (which occupy only some 25 — 30 of the 168 hours in the week). The Undergraduate Research Opportunities Programme (UROP) gives undergraduates the chance to: learn at first hand about the sort of activities they can expect to undertake after graduating; learn at their own pace without formal instruction; gain realistic writing experience; have the opportunity of contributing to knowledge in their subject; decide whether or not to go into a particular field of work; develop interests which they bring from outside the college, from industrial experience, from technical hobbies, and so on; cross disciplinary boundaries; develop self-confidence; learn self-discipline in time and priorities; become more genuinely part of the academic community by meeting staff and postgraduates informally in contexts where no one feels embarrassed; achieve a publication, prototype, invention, prize, or other tangible item; sometimes earn marks or money; almost always be inspired concerning the context and purpose of their formal coursework.

For the staff an undergraduate research opportunities scheme can offer: additional help in the laboratory or library; the chance to test the feasibility of risky ideas not suitable for research students; an opportunity to develop rudimentary ideas prior to a grant application for research support (to strengthen the application); considerable intellectual stimulus in making complex ideas accessible to the undergraduates; improvement in the quality and achievement of formal projects included within the regular curriculum; improved recruitment of postgraduate students;

additional tangible professional development such as publications; and inexpensive expansion of the scope and variety of research undertaken. The MIT scheme, which has been in operation for over ten years, is run on a very modest budget and in the 'spare time' of the staff. At present, over two-thirds of the undergraduates and over two-thirds of the staff are involved with the scheme at any one time. Similar schemes have recently been established at Imperial College and at the University of Aston.

Activities such as these are, we would argue, extremely important if students are to experience the world of 'telegrams and anger' from which problems emerge which are sufficiently challenging to absorb their intellectual energies. To facilitate this type of encounter it may be necessary for staff to cut down the number of hours of formal contact with students — to shift emphasis from the delivery of instruction by staff to the reading for a degree by students.

To accommodate the great range of interests and abilities of students in higher education, it will be necessary to give even more attention than has hitherto been given to establishing effective means of absorbing students into action agencies (hospitals, factories, theatres, law offices, town planning offices, etc.). We therefore make our next proposition.

Proposition 2.4
A feasibility study should be carried out concerning the possibility of action agencies having education officers on their staff, paid for if necessary from DES funds, whose tasks would be to draw students into the agencies for the practical part of their studies and to arrange interchange of senior personnel.

It may well be argued that, particularly in times of financial stress, action agencies (hospitals, factories, and so on) have enough to cope with without trying to accommodate students for the practical, experiential component of their studies. Difficult though the task may be (and industrial tutors are already finding sandwich placements harder and harder to secure), it is essential that it be tackled. It will be futile to complain that students are unfitted for the world of work or that they lack operational styles of thinking (the desire and capacity to tackle practical problems) if they have not been given the chance to get inside places of work outside their higher education institutions where they can the more readily develop these styles of thinking.

Education officers on the staff of action agencies could have responsibility, inter alia, for: finding work within the action agency for students coming for periods ranging from an afternoon a week to a six-month sandwich placement; writing handbooks (with leading questions about what to look out for) to help students profit from their practical work; reading and criticizing reports, essays, dissertations by students; ensuring that reports by students on problems to which solutions had been proposed reached the appropriate people within the action agency; visiting the students' home institutions to talk with the teaching staff (attending curriculum planning committees, examiners meetings, and those occasions which permit relaxed, informal contact — rites of passage as staff and students come and go, etc.); carrying out systematic evaluation of the impact of the practical placement on students' academic thinking, career intentions and personal values.

If it is assumed that students would benefit by intercalated periods of practical activity and academic reflection, it may also be assumed that staff would benefit in like manner. It could be an additional part of an education officer's job to arrange interchange of personnel at all levels, including the highest, with secondments from the action agencies to higher education (or, as is already common, participation in seminars) and of personnel from higher education to industry (again as already occurs to some extent). In short, the education officers would be animateurs responsible for encouraging interaction between higher education institutions and action agencies at all levels.

It follows from what we have suggested that the proposed education officers would have to be of the very highest calibre. Ideally they would need to have both academic experience (to be able to sense the academic potential of particular exercises) and experience in the action agencies (to be credible and acceptable to the people with whom they would be working).

We are fully aware of the potential cost of what we propose. We believe, however, that much could be achieved without significant additional cost by a radical deployment of existing higher education personnel. If, in addition, the existing posts in industry of training officer were upgraded (to include not only the induction of unskilled and semi-skilled workers but also people undergoing higher education), a formidable impact could be made upon the experiential component of higher education.

One caveat: in any scheme promoting experiential learning it would be important for the education officers to guard against 'substitution' — the replacement by subsidized labour of work by which other people would normally earn their living. The important economic argument in favour of experiential learning is that students are 'paid' already in the sense that their basic living expenses are met. Any work which they do should be an addition to what is already possible in the action agency and, thereby, produce an overall increase in productivity. For example, in the version of experiential learning known as study service (cf Goodlad 1982), students can carry out surveys which could not otherwise be undertaken, spend time with physically or mentally handicapped people with a view to teaching them skills with which to become less dependent, assist teachers in mixed ability classes with either very bright or very backward pupils (through tutoring, which, it must be emphasized, is not teaching but a supplement to teaching), design and make one-off systems or devices for the handicapped, and so on.

One of the most important opportunities offered by experiential learning of all sorts is that of learning about careers and of seeing how the theoretical components of disciplines influence and are influenced by the world of practical affairs. It may seem a paradox that such work which is highly specific should be most commended for its general educational potential; but this is the value we attach to it. It follows, therefore, that opportunities for experiential learning should be available in students' early years of higher education, rather than in their final years, and, of course, in secondary schooling too.

The phenomenon of 'academic drift (cf Neave 1979) is relevant here. Although in action agencies subjects may become more and more practical (possibly even losing contact with co-ordinating Theory and explicit concern with social accountability), in higher education institutions academic subjects have a constant tendency to become more and more theoretical; thus engineering moves towards physics and mathematics, medicine moves towards physiology and biochemistry, social work moves towards, variously, psychology or political science, and so on. Behind this phenomenon lies the reward system for academics where security of tenure, promotion, and, above all, 'international visibility' are achieved through publication. Until this reward system changes (and it is difficult to see how it will when fame is the spur), academics will tend to try to make their students as much like themselves as possible. We have argued above (page 75) that for academics to offer any intellectual role model other than themselves would be inauthentic and smacking of 'bad faith'; certainly, if more academics are really fired by their studies, they will be passionately eager to kindle fires in the imaginations of their students. The consequence of this is that academic courses tend to become more and more specialized: third-year options in special areas are needed to give undergraduates a taste of what postgraduate work might be like; second-year studies seem too vague and general unless they involve significant preparation for the third-year options; a few hours of lectures in the second year are hardly adequate for this purpose — better, therefore, to do away with the generalist first year and let students go straight into their specialisms. So great is the amount of material to be 'covered' that it then seems tempting to encourage students to take specialist GCE 'A' levels — electronics, economics, sociology, and so on. On schools the pressure mounts to offer a multiplicity of 'A' level courses (30 is not unusual in large comprehensive schools) with attendant logistic problems in the deployment of teachers — (with the effect that lower-school classes are often unacceptably large). In short, the understandable desire of academics for international visibility, attainable primarily through publication in highly specialized areas, produces a cascade effect through the educational system emphasizing greater and greater specialization. We believe that this is damaging.

We have already indicated how, through undergraduate research opportunities programmes, academics can involve undergraduates in research and consultancy of direct practical value and with even the most arcane research to the profit of both academics and the students. We argue below (pages 94ff) that with a greater use of project work, enormous flexibility of studies could be achieved. To allow students in higher education adequate time for reflection, and the chance to make wise choices of their higher level studies, and to draw into specialist studies only those who are really committed to them, we advocate a two-year general course, leading to the Bachelors degree, as the basic component of higher education, with access to professional and Masters degree courses (normally 2 years) restricted according to national requirements.

THE FLEXIBILITY OF GENERAL AND SPECIALIST COURSES

Proposition 3.1
Entry into higher education should be made less dependent on examination success in specialist subjects.

British universities are required to bring their students up to the international standard for professional employment in a time shorter than is thought possible in almost any other advanced country. Mathematicians, scientists, engineers and doctors rely on a severely specialized sixth-form curriculum which may indeed provide a good education but only for some pupils, and by accident rather than design. Certainly these courses are not regarded as educational in a general sense; very few students opt for them except with a specialist career in mind.

The problem is accentuated by the too-frequently indifferent quality of school teaching in mathematics and physics which must surely turn away undecided pupils into better-taught and initially less demanding innumerate subjects. Yet there is a great need in management and administration for non-specialists who are reasonably well informed about scientific attitudes, and can read a balance-sheet or endure a scientific presentation without suffering instant mental paralysis. It would equally benefit the country and individual students if science at school acquired the reputation of being an exciting subject, worthy of the attention of imaginative boys and girls alike.

To achieve this end universities must cease to expect a high level of specialism at entry. As a corollary students should not be expected to commit themselves to their specialism until they have taken some first-year courses and discovered their aptitudes and desires. It is probably only in this country that a student can find himself irrevocably set on the path of, say, engineering before entering higher education and seeing what is involved. We suggest that it is better for a student to have conceived an interest in science through a limited introduction at school to any science whatever by an enthusiastic teacher, than to have suffered second-rate teaching (which may have to be untaught later) and carry on reluctantly in the subject because he has already burnt his boats. It would mean, of course, that the first year at university would find him less advanced than now; but he should be all the better for that in the end. Those who aimed at professional employment would proceed to at least one year's postgraduate training. The overall cost would be rather more than the present cut-price training, but the advantage aimed at — to make scientific and technological courses more attractive at the secondary level — is something worth paying for.

This proposal is an evolutionary measure; a revolutionary measure attacking the problem at a more fundamental level is outlined in Proposition 3.3.

Proposition 3.2
At each critical point in the educational system, the nature and content of courses should be primarily determined by the needs of those who are leaving education at that point.

There is a generalization of the principle underlying Proposition 8. Those who continue in formal education have the opportunity to correct imbalances in their earlier experience. Thus, universities should see their task as receiving students who have been educated at school as if they were finishing their education at eighteen, and providing the best opportunity for them to develop their talents further. They should not devise courses and set examinations as if only those who get firsts and proceed to research are important. Those responsible for the later stages in education should avoid, as far as possible, putting pressure on the earlier stages.

Proposition 3.3
Existing 3-year specialized university courses should be replaced by 2-year general courses. Student grants should be available very widely for these two years, but the numbers supported on advanced courses might be broadly influenced by the need for specialists. Such a radical change cannot be carried through without extensive preliminary work.

The radical proposal (Swann 1968; Pippard 1972) which has been most fully (though still only schematically) developed to meet the requirement for a less specialized, science-based education, which nevertheless can satisfy the need for a professional training, is the so-called 2 + 2 system. Since it was conceived with the problem of the professional specialist in mind, it is best described in these terms; at the end we shall indicate how it might be meshed in with non-specialist courses. In this scheme the first two years are seen to be primarily general rather than vocational, so that the greatest attention is paid to developing a wide range of interests and an alert response, constructive and critical, to the sort of problem that an educated non-specialist may be expected to tackle in the normal course of his career. Instruction is by lecture (and practical work if needed), supplemented by discussion groups (seminars) in which the art of rational analysis is developed, and by tutorials in which the individual student may seek help.

In order to clarify the exposition, the following section describes a hypothetical general course occupying two-thirds of the first two years, together with some logistic details. It is easier to demolish such a course syllabus than to create one, and we wish to stress that we attach no special value to this particular syllabus. It is conceivable that in some university there would be found scientists, lawyers, historians and economists who would see it as matching what they would like to present. Our aim, however, is not to impose syllabuses, but to encourage teachers from different disciplines to talk together until they find out how they can co-operate in leading their students towards a constructive intelligent appreciation of real issues.

The course outlined below is to be thought of as one of a number, perhaps fifteen, offered by a university accepting 1,800 new students a year, so that a typical course would attract 120. The course would run for two years, with about 120 lectures in each year, together with seminars, tutorials and (if appropriate) a strictly limited amount of laboratory work. Given a 25-week teaching year, there would be about five lectures a week — not too light (when supplemented by another, possibly more vocational course of about half this weight) to arouse suspicion of disgraceful idleness, yet light enough for the enthusiast to find ample time to devote his attention to other subjects, especially if his heart is set on gaining acceptance to specialist third and fourth year courses.

URBAN TECHNOLOGY

The theme running through the course is the transformation of towns and cities between about 1840 and the present day as a consequence of scientific and technological development including electricity, gas, roads, sewers and telephones.

Course A (120 lectures)
Basic science, taught rather discursively (ie with some emphasis on historical development, social relations of science, public support and public education in science, funding of research, especially the differences that have taken place in 100 years). The important areas would be electricity, thermodynamics, hydraulics and soil science, much of the last two at the level of a course in physical geography. There should be a strong technological bias towards, for example, dynamics, heat engines. Practical work associated

with this course would be designed to illuminate ideas rather than teach technical skills.

Course B (30 lectures)
Economics

Course C (30 lectures)
General principles underlying economics and law, the problems of long-term capital investment, and the processes of civil law. The illustrations should not be confined to urban technology, though a limited number of examples might be included.

Course D (60 lectures)
Social history, 1840 — present day, including extended illustration and discussion of public dependence on utilities and an examination of modern crises of confidence (alternative society, energy crisis and nuclear power, automation and unemployment).

This course, D, is central in tying together the ideas in the others, and it is this course that should generate most seminar discussions and extended essays.

With 120 students in each of two years, 240 in all, but counting as two-thirds, ie 160 full-time equivalents, one might expect to find the equivalent of fourteen lecturers assigned to the course. Each would give an average of seventeen lectures a year and take tutorial and seminar responsibilty for seventeen students (half in each year). Thus with seminar groups of eight to nine, each student could attend one seminar a week, or, with groups of seventeen, two a week, and the lecturer would be conducting two a week, one for each year. Similarly, if tutorials were given in groups of four, each lecturer would take responsibility for four groups; he would not necessarily teach them all, since research students provide invaluable help. This does not seem an excessive teaching load; in practice it would usually be spread among a large number of staff who would be partly engaged in teaching specialist courses as well.

The student whose ultimate aim is professional qualification will be spending half his time in this general course on scientific matters, and in addition a third of his time on a supplementary science course. This adds up to two-thirds of his time spent on science. If he proceeds to two years on advanced work, he finishes having spent three and a third years on science, with four years in which to digest the concepts. Thus the 2 + 2 scheme permits sound scientific and technical training, very little (if at all) inferior to three undergraduate years plus one year MSc.

With this as an example, the following points should serve to clarify the intentions and organization of the scheme.

It is a coherent course, assembled round a unifying theme, which enables each separate strand of special knowledge to be presented both as a discipline and as a useful tool.

In contrast to an à la carte menu of optional courses from which a student might select arbitrarily, the university assumes the responsibility of indicating what disciplines may be usefully married so as to leave the student with a sense of purpose in what he has learned. The judgement involved is something most students cannot easily make for themselves at the outset, and the senior staff may properly deploy their experience in this matter. So long as each university offers a variety of integrated general courses, and different universities take pride in being different in their offerings, there is no danger of doctrinaire conditioning of the students.

The coherence of the course ensures that the groups of students constituting the seminars have a common background, so that problems for discussion may be chosen so as to involve everyone equally. Precisely how a seminar should be conducted must depend on the seminar leader, a staff member, and on the topic but, again purely as a concrete example, one might envisage something like the following in the Urban Technology course. The topic is selected by the leader — should the city centre be made a pedestrian precinct, and if so how shall it be funded and what public transport should be provided? Available written material is provided for study; the early discussions serve to reveal the need for more material and more on-the-spot investigations; decisions are made about who shall do the work and by what date; ultimately a report is written, with firm recommendations for action. The task of the leaders throughout the whole process is not to instruct but to maintain the level of discourse — to ensure that difficulties are not covered up during the development of the argument, but equally that the final report is crisp in its recommendations and does not (in traditional academic fashion) defer decision for yet more work to be done. This method encourages teamwork and responsibility among students. The groups do not require the continual presence of a teacher and can, therefore, be used with larger than normal tutorial classes (cf the syndicate method (Collier 1968, 1969)).

It would enhance the value of the seminars if, at the conclusion, one or more students from each seminar in a particular group presented their report at an assembly of all the students and seminar leaders involved (eg 120 students, 7-14 reports). Critical discussion would be encouraged, and the best effort chosen by popular vote.

The best reports should be made available in libraries, and exchanged between universities, to build up a corpus of good examples that would encourage acceptance of this form of education as normal (as was done in the General Education in Engineering (GEE) project — see Goodlad 1977). The institution of prizes, within universities or even on a national scale, would further encourage whole-hearted participation.

It may be objected that general courses have never worked. In the United States, however, they do; even mathematicians, who in this country are supposed to mature so young that no time must be wasted in developing their talent, accept the yoke of general education and in the event do not seem any the worse as mathematicians. The essential point is that we have never attempted to give all students a general education — general courses have been but one option in parallel with specialization, and the latter has attracted an overwhelming proportion of the most talented students. There is no reason to suppose that once a change had been made in all universities to a scheme in which general courses were the accepted staple, they would be resented any more than in the US.

It is not envisaged that the general courses would comprise the whole of the first two years' work; they might notionally take up two-thirds of the available time, leaving the student free to study a special topic if he wished to proceed to a further intensive specialization, or some other non-vocational pursuit (a foreign language, for example). He might even become involved in directed community work, such as coaching pupils at a local school (see Proposition 2.2).

Public support must be dependent on his taking the general course seriously. One might hope to see the minimum standard for entry set quite low, so that as many as wished to continue their general education would be permitted to do so and supported for two years. During this time they would be able to discover what they wanted to do under much better conditions than at school, since they would be mixing with students on advanced specialist courses and could appraise their own suitability for the intellectual discipline involved.

To gain public support on an advanced course the student would need, first, to obtain a qualifying mark in his general course and, secondly, to be accepted by the department running the advanced course. His performance in whatever subject he was studying in parallel with the general course might well be the critical factor here. Selection at this stage is likely to be fairer than that based only upon school data.

In contrast to the first two years, which should be thrown as wide open as possible, the numbers taking advanced courses (typically a further two years) could be strictly limited and entry made competitive. To aid the process of selection, the advanced courses should be severe, even punishing, in their intellectual demands so that the numbers seeking entry did not greatly exceed the places available. Since the purpose of the advanced courses is primarily vocational training there need be no qualms about expecting the highest standards of application from those who choose to take them.

All institutions of higher education, not solely universities, would have a part to play in advanced courses.

The preceding account has been couched in terms of a science-based general course, since the 2 + 2 scheme was primarily conceived as a way of promoting general scientific literacy without lowering the standard of professional training. There seems to be no reason in principle why it should not be adopted also for non-scientific professions (architecture, law, economics), as well as for the humanities. In the latter, it must be admitted, the need for two-year advanced courses is more limited, but it is very real if essential scholarship is not to wither.

Any proposal of this nature is guaranteed criticism from a substantial number of academics who see the three-year Bachelors degree as a sacred institution — it is only in their third year, they say, that students begin to appreciate the point of a university or polytechnic. We submit that it is only in their *last* year, whatever year that may be, that this enlightenment dawns. Other countries have different lengths of course, and very different standards of degrees, and one should not despair of getting used to a new length and a new standard once they become the norm. For this reason we do not hesitate to propose that the two-year general course deserves the award of a Bachelors degree, and the advanced course the Masters degree.

Proposition 3.4
Each year of each student's curriculum should provide for a student's own project.

Whatever they may lack in disciplinary coherence, projects have been found to give students a sense of personal achievement, to let them see how subjects hold together and to synthesize knowledge from various sources (cf SRHE 1975). If, as we argue below (Proposition 4.1), academic excellence involves the capacity to make connections (rather than being limited to knowledge of specifics), it is important that students be given exercises which involve making connections and achieving an individual synthesis of ideas. Many departments already provide for a student's own project in the final year of study. We would argue that, particularly if a 2 + 2 system is introduced, it would be valuable to provide for projects in each year of study. Interestingly, although single-subject Honours degree courses are sometimes criticized as being too specialized, students often find them to be not specialized enough. Students' experience of curricula is often of a sequence of short (30-lecture) courses on various topics with the connections between topics being neglected or left to chance. An aim of project work would be to invite the student to make connections between the parts of a single-subject curriculum or between the main discipline and others.

Project methods are sometimes resisted on the grounds that assessment may be a problem with different students on a single course (who have to be ranked for degree Honours classes) being engaged on projects of varying technical or conceptual difficulty. We believe that it is possible to allow for the variations of difficulty involved in the projects and that the modes of assessment commonly used to assess research are both applicable to undergraduate projects and well known to most academics. That is to say, projects are not judged solely on the specific facts they contain but rather on: internal consistency; relating of ideas to central preoccupations within a discipline or field of enquiry; range and quality of information used; familiarity with previous work; sensitivity to the potential of the ideas discussed for future work; etc. We believe, in fact, that greater use of projects (or other methods which rely more on a student's own initiative than on input from teachers) may produce a movement in favour of a new definition of academic excellence.

PROFESSIONAL STANDARDS AND ASSESSMENT

Proposition 4.1.
Assessment in higher education should reflect a conception of academic excellence as involving the ability to think to some purpose.

It is sometimes maintained that the fundamental raison d'etre of higher education is 'the pursuit of excellence'; but often it is not clear precisely what is meant by excellence. We have recommended (Proposition 2.1 above) that curricula in higher education should where possible and appropriate encourage in students an action-oriented, operational style of thinking. It follows that we would wish to see conceptions of excellence reflecting the ability to think to some purpose embodied within schedules of assessment, not least because, as Snyder (1971) and others have demonstrated, the explicit curriculum may be less important to students than the 'hidden curriculum' which is largely determined by the type(s) of assessment used.

In what follows, we have in mind particularly notions of excellence as they apply to the direct preparation of students for professional life; and we have in a — d below quoted directly from the work of William Birch. We do, however, believe that many points are equally applicable to academic studies which, although contextually relevant to various occupations, are not necessarily conceived as preparation for professions. We would hope, too, that the first two years of a 2 + 2 structure of studies would inculcate sensitivity to the ways in which disciplines (based on forms of academic theory) illuminate fields of inquiry (with all the multi-dimensional incoherence that everyday issues involve). We hope, therefore, that in what follows readers will interpret the word 'profession' widely.

Academic excellence, we would argue, involves most if not all of the following:

a As clear an understanding of the conceptual basis of a student's professional field as its nature and the state of its development permits
b An appropriate grasp of the relevant academic disciplines and their inter-relationships (the knowledge base) such that students can:
   i bring to bear on professional problems the available theoretical

insights and methods of analysis, and
  ii sustain and develop their grasp of the knowledge base of their profession and its relationships to practice
 c An ability to integrate theory and practice through the study of problems which have been 'solved' and thus to acquire:
   i the self-confidence which comes from practice, and
   ii the basis for exercising sound professional judgements
 d An ability to recognize and to formulate, in a manner which permits some approach to a solution, significant new problems within their professional field
 e The ability to write clear, readable, and accurate English
 f The ability to handle ideas with a high level of conceptual density
 g The ability to organize large quantities of data
 h The ability to make a sensible limitation of a field of inquiry to permit precision of observation (and, when necessary, effective action)
 i An ability to enjoy the work and to communicate that enjoyment to other people
 j The ability to penetrate to the nub of a complex, multi-dimensional issue.

Few of the dimensions of excellence listed above involve knowledge of specific facts, important though that may be. Our intention is to permit and encourage the maximum possible *flexibility* in how learning is acquired, how excellence is achieved. It is possible, indeed probable, that most students will wish to accept the curricula provided by higher education institutions as and when they are offered. Our concern, however, is to suggest conditions which permit freedom of movement within and between curricula, and institutions, for students in full- or part-time attendance. (The issue of credit transfer is involved here, though we have not dealt with it explicitly). In our judgement, flexible arrangements for *assessment* are the key to this, and assessment in turn depends upon clear perception of the broad competencies (not just knowledge of specific facts) which are to be assessed.

Higher education is much more than assimilating predigested knowledge and reproducing it under examination conditions; every aspect that is recognized as important should be assessed, so as to emphasize to the student its importance, and have it carry an appropriate weight in whatever final evaluation the higher education institution presents to the public. However detailed the information released and however difficult the reconciliation of different grades achieved by any one student in different parts of the assessment, the institution has a responsibility to award some simple, overall mark of quality. This is what most employers want, and many are in a position to demand. When eligibility for a research grant, a teaching post, a civil service appointment, has come to be determined by the class of final degree, any decision to stop awarding such a classmark will throw the burden of decision onto the shoulders of an administrative official who is even less likely than a board of examiners to relish the task of exercising wise judgement, and certainly less well-informed about each individual case.

It is not only the employer, however, who requires unambiguous advice from the examiners; the majority of students understandably wish to know what weight each part of the curriculum carries. It should be made clear that in so delicate a process as assessing a final class (which may be critical to a graduate's career prospects) a simple aggregation of marks leads to a very rough sort of justice. Admittedly, for the examiners to use their skill and experience to make significant adjustments to the order revealed by the aggregate, results in some uncertainty as to their criteria. It can also prolong examiners' meetings when debate develops about how far an exceptional project shall be allowed to compensate for indifferent paperwork. But the examiners will probably carry out their task best if they look on themselves as representatives of the world their graduates are about to enter. The qualities demanded of a scientist or other professional in industry are not markedly different from what an academic hopes to find in his research students — knowledge, imagination, integrity, etc. — and if examiners find that they cannot assess and balance these qualities it is the method of assessment and/or the nature of the courses that should be faulted. Something is seriously amiss if higher education institutions are blamed by employers for producing first-class graduates who are no use — and if this happens the higher education institution should anxiously examine their own procedures. This is the sort of argument that should be explained to students regularly, until it becomes part of the climate of the higher education institution to realize that there are many roads to success and that the examiners' purpose is not to lay down a rigorous plan for all to follow, but to indicate a norm and to study sensitively the credentials of those whose talents do not easily fit.

Is the single class mark all that a higher education institution should publish? This is a difficult problem, since clearly to make a complete transcript available in addition to the class would result in embarrassing comparisons and almost certainly in lawsuits. Perhaps certain items of information should be available: eg whether the student undertook a project and, if so, what class it was awarded. Each institution, each faculty even, would have to decide its policy in this matter. It is not necessary that the information be broadcast, but if it is to be recorded for the purpose of testimonials the student should be informed of the nature of the record. (For a valuable discussion of this issue, see Rowntree 1977.)

Proposition 4.2
Whenever possible, higher education institutions should state what is to be assessed rather than how and when students are to learn.

The writing of course objectives is notoriously difficult. Broad goals and aims are often written in such vague phraseology as not to indicate how it would be possible to determine whether or not they had been achieved. By contrast, objectives written in behavioural terms (as followers of B.S. Bloom (1956) would advocate) can trivialize teaching and learning and reduce pattern to incoherence. In our judgement, a clear and comprehensive account of what is to be assessed and how presupposes that course goals, aims, and detailed objectives have been worked out with care. In the interests of flexibility, we would recommend a much fuller statement of what is to be assessed than is usual in higher education.

First, the convention of writing a syllabus in a few enigmatic lines constrains students to attend lectures and other classes simply to find out the content of the course on which they are going to be assessed. (Lecturers may also never have faced the discipline of thinking through what they are really trying to do.) Brilliant students can become bored; weaker students sometimes cannot follow classes which are, of necessity, aimed at some notional middle-ability students. Huge amounts of staff and student time can be used up in inefficient activity in which both staff and students may be colluding in the belief that the 'busy-work' involved is real work.

Secondly, the tram-lining by timetable (which follows from inadequate specification of what is to be assessed) prevents express routes and slow lanes from being adopted which might free able students or less able students respectively to move through the curriculum at their own paces. There is no reason to suppose that students would avoid classes; but the clear specification of what is to be learned would at least give them some choice in the matter.

Thirdly, while we are not in favour of courses which are modular in *content* (with a cafeteria or à la carte provision), we see no reason why courses should not be modular in *timing;* that is to say, students could, indeed should, be able to move through a table d'hote curriculum, planned to provide a required sequence, in their own time, without necessarily relying on the convoying which lack of clear statements involves. Part-time students might be greatly aided by such an approach. As the cost of full-time study rises (a significant portion being absorbed in maintenance allowances for full-time students), part-time study may become increasingly attractive. Similarly, part-time study, as the Open University has abundantly demonstrated, is attractive to mature students (who may not be able, or may not wish, to relinquish family or work responsibilities) or to others seeking continuing education.

Administration might be facilitated if the income of higher education institutions was attached to students *assessed* rather than students in attendance. Institutions could charge one fee to represent the full costs of assessment and an additional fee for those availing themselves of specific forms of instruction. To reinforce this point, we put forward Proposition 4.3.

Proposition 4.3
Professional institutions and the CNAA should offer to assess anyone prepared to pay the assessment fees and should not also require attendance at specific courses.

As we have indicated above (page 89), our broad goal is to encourage as many people as possible to get as much education as they would like by whatever means possible throughout their lives. At present, achieving academic qualifications (undoubtedly a powerful incentive to study (cf Collins 1979 and Dore 1976)) is largely linked to attending specific courses. The consequence is that people who could be autodidacts or who might benefit from the incentive to *study* offered by the potential award of qualifications are denied the opportunity to better themselves because they may be unwilling or unable to free themselves (or pay) for the courses of *tuition* offered.

To urge this loosening of the system (this removal almost of certain restrictive practices), does not imply that we do not highly value full-time courses with all that residence has to offer. There may, indeed, be educational value in the very process of going to college — whatever is (or is not) studied. All we are recommending is a modest alteration of arrangements to encourage maximum participation in *learning* — for which we would argue specific *teaching* is not always necessary.

A shift of emphasis towards assessment (and away from specific institutional contexts for learning) would facilitate mixed modes of study — some full-time, some part-time; some by attendance at courses, some by distance-learning; and so on.

TOWARDS PROFESSIONAL FLEXIBILITY

Proposition 5.1
Procedures should be examined, both at system and at institution level, to secure the possibility of curriculum innovation.

At present, curriculum innovation within higher education institutions is severely inhibited because nearly all funds are allotted to existing departments. More seriously, during the present economic recession, at the very time when adventurous ideas should be being encouraged, the gross uncertainty of planning is proving a conservative influence. Certainly the UGC (at system level) and individual colleges (at institution level) can be flexible in using the funds made available to them; but at present pressures are in favour of preserving the status quo rather than in favour of generating an entrepreneurial atmosphere in higher education. What follows may seem outrageously optimistic; but we are comforted by the recollection that the Beveridge report, laying the foundations for the Welfare State, was written during the Second World War!

To achieve a certain minimal stability of educational planning, it is a matter of some urgency that government propose a basic level of funding at today's prices on a five-yearly basis each year — the so-called rolling quinquennium. The basic figure (which should, of course, be proposed both for the university and local authority controlled sectors) should be a minimum guaranteed figure (which could be below current funding levels), so that planning can be undertaken without the massive and damaging shifts of policy introduced by changing governments. In short, a minimal level of funding should effectively be 'taken out of politics', with only levels of supplementation being regularly reviewed. Such an expedient would secure for government the possibility of radical changes in the funding of higher education — but with a built-in time-lag of five years.

The UGC, and whatever body comes in due course to oversee the funding of other sectors of higher education, should seek to establish an uncommitted reserve of funds within a basic (minimal) allocation to be bid for by institutions on a competitive basis. It would be important to secure the provision that funds allocated to institutions on this basis would not need to be used in the year in which they were granted but rather within, say, seven years — to permit and encourage thoughtful planning, running, and evaluation of new degree courses.

Likewise, individual institutions should be encouraged by the UGC, and other funding bodies, to build up uncommitted reserves of their own, again to be bid for on a competitive basis by individual (or groups of) faculty members on an institution-wide basis. This measure might be expected to loosen the hold on existing curricula of existing departments and to foster innovations which cut across departmental and/or disciplinary boundaries.

Although at present the notion will undoubtedly strike many people as unthinkable, we would welcome a feasibility study (based perhaps on a pilot programme in two or more institutions) of offering academic staff a minimum guaranteed salary (with associated minimum requirements of teaching hours) and permitting staff to make up additional earnings by taking on additional teaching (or research contracts or consultancy) as their interests and competencies indicated. If this idea were linked to the establishing of uncommitted reserves within institutions and at system level, considerable encouragement might be given to rapidly developing subjects in which degree programmes are undoubtedly needed — such as microelectronics and biotechnology.

Proposition 5.2
Research is needed into several areas which vitally affect curricula.

There are abundant policy issues which require independent study on a pretty massive scale. For example, the independence of higher education institutions is significantly eroded by the detailed prescriptions given by many professional validating bodies for what students must know to gain exemption from various professional qualifying examinations. Institutions which ignored these prescriptions would rapidly go out of business. The Privy Council issues charters to these bodies; yet it is not clear on what basis it does so nor by what principles, and with what theories of instruction and/or professional practice, the validating bodies draw up their syllabus details. Much needs to be known about the purposes and procedures of these bodies and how they interact with higher education institutions. The subject is one of such major importance that a hit-and-run conventional academic research project would be much less valuable than, as it were, a continuing commission with powers to initiate policy discussions and make recommendations for change as it went about its work.

Secondly, the interface of higher education with teaching at secondary school level might require extended study. If a more operational, problem-oriented perspective emerged in higher education along the lines we recommend, it might be desirable for schooling to be shaped in a similar manner. Not only do the skills of applying knowledge take time to develop (indicating the value of starting the process in schools rather than in higher education), but also we believe that a more operational approach to learning might enhance the employment prospects for 16 to 19-year-old pupils, help with motivation problems in schools, and constitute a suitable preparation for the sort of 2 + 2 system we have outlined above (under Proposition 3.3). Bligh (1981), for example, has sketched the possible organization of secondary school curricula in terms of six faculties as follows:

1 *Communication* to include English and foreign languages, art, film, and music. 2 *Mathematics, Computing, and Logic*. 3 *Health* to include medicine, biology, gardening, agriculture, and physical education. 4 *Engineering and Technology* to include the physical sciences, inquiry, invention, and design. 5 *Decision Making* to include management, systems thinking, administration, environmental planning, home management, accountancy, ethics, as well as social studies, history, politics, sociology, industrial relations, law, organizations, and economics. 6 *Personal Relations* to include study of individual development, parenthood, career development, education, family care, and the interaction of individuals in groups.

In this programme, emphasis is shifted from (what dominates at present) knowledge to skills. The underlying intention is not to subvert or diminish the imaginative power and delight inherent in many existing school studies, but rather to present them in a context which is manifestly purposeful and related at as many points as possible with the lives children lead outside school.

Thirdly, research is needed to discover how curricula take their present shape and how individuals or groups not at present represented in the planning or provision of higher education can make their views carry weight. There is abundant evidence (cf Fulton 1981; Halsey, Heath and Ridge 1980) that postwar educational reforms have not produced an equitable distribution of higher education by social class. Similarly, there is growing evidence (cf The Runnymede Trust 1980) that the children of immigrants coming into Britain may not be appropriately provided for in the educational system. It is possible that under-represented groups may not find in existing higher education anything to command their interest. If we are to avoid cultural reproduction of the most oppressive kind (cf Bourdieu and Passeron 1977) we need to examine new ways of arranging for the curriculum of higher education to reflect social and intellectual movements in society.

Each of these three examples — validation, the interface between schooling and higher education, and cultural reproduction — involve issues of such complexity and importance that small-scale research and development exercises are unlikely to have much impact. To address these and all the numerous other issues in higher education meriting research (institutional financing and management, cognitive and ethical development in students, methods of learning and teaching, strategies for disseminating research findings, etc.) we believe that a major initiative is now urgently needed.

REFERENCES

Barrows, H.S. & Tamblyn, R. (1980) *Problem-Based Learning: an approach to medical education* New York: Springer

Bell, Daniel (1966) *The Reforming of General Education* London: Columbia University Press

Birch, W.B. (1981) *The Changing Relationship between Higher Education and Working Life* Unpublished paper presented to OECD, Paris, October 1981

Bligh, D.A. (1981) *Some Gropings towards a Radical Synthesis* Unpublished paper. Teaching Services Centre, University of Exeter

Bloom, B.S. et al. (1956) *Taxonomy of Educational Objectives* London: Longman

Bourdieu, P. and Passeron, J.C. (1977) *Reproduction in Education, Society, and Culture* translated by R. Nice. London: Sage

Boyer, E.L. and Levine, A. (1981) *A Quest for Common Learning* Washington DC: Carnegie Foundation for the Advancement of Teaching

Brown, J. & Goodlad, S. (1974) Community related project work in engineering. In Goodlad, S. (Editor) *Education and Social Action* Chapter 6. London: George Allen and Unwin

CERI (1972) *Interdisciplinarity: Problems of teaching and research in universities* Centre for Educational Research and Innovation,

Organization for Economic Cooperation and Development, Paris
Chickering, A.W. (1977) *Experience and Learning: An introduction to Experiential Learning* New York: Change Magazine Press
Collier, K.G. (1968) *New Dimensions in Higher Education* London: Longman
Collier, K.G. (1969) Syndicate methods: further evidence and comment *Universities Quarterly* 23 (4)
Collins, R. (1979) *The Credential Society* New York and London: Academic Press
CNAA (Annually) *Directory of First Degree Courses* London: Council for National Academic Awards
Daiches, D. (Editor) (1964) *The Idea of a New University* London: Andre Deutsch
Dore, R. (1976) *The Diploma Disease: Education, Qualification, and Development* London: George Allen and Unwin
Duley, J.S. (1981) Field experience education. In A. W. Chickering (Editor) *The Modern American College* San Francisco and London: Jossey Bass
Finniston, M. (1980) *Engineering our Future* Report of the Committee of Inquiry into the Engineering Profession. Cmnd. 7794. London: HMSO
Fulton, O. (Editor) (1981) *Access to Higher Education* Guildford: Society for Research into Higher Education
Goodlad, S. (1976) *Conflict and Consensus in Higher Education* London: Hodder & Stoughton Educational
Goodlad, S. (1977) *SocioTechnical Projects in Engineering Education* University of Stirling: General Education in Engineering (GEE) Project
Goodlad, S. (1979) *Learning by Teaching: An introduction to tutoring* London: Community Service Volunteers
Goodlad, S. (Editor) (1982) *Study Service: An examination of community service as a method of study in higher education* Windsor: NFER Nelson
Halsey, A.H., Heath, A.F. and Ridge, J.M. (1980) *Origins and Destinations. Family, Class, and Education in Modern Britain.* Oxford: Clarendon Press
Harvard Committee (1945) *General Education in a Free Society* Cambridge, Massachusetts: Harvard University Press
Hirst, P.H. (1974) *Knowledge and the Curriculum* London: Routledge & Kegan Paul
Kaysen, C. (Editor) (1973) *Content and Context. Essays on College Education* A report prepared for the Carnegie Commission in Higher Education. London: McGraw Hill, London
Kuhn, T.S. (1970) *The Structure of Scientific Revolutions* (2nd edn) University of Chicago Press (1962)
MacVicar, M.L.A. (1976) *UROP What's it all about?* The MIT Undergraduate Research Opportunities Programme, 1969/1976. Cambridge, Massachusetts: Massachusetts Institute of Technology

Minogue, K.R. (1973) *The Concept of a University* London: Weidenfeld and Nicolson

Neave, G. (1979) Academic drift: some views from Europe *Studies in Higher Education* 4 (2) 143-159

Niblett, W.R. (Editor) (1974) *Universities Between Two Worlds* London: University of London Press

Niblett, W.R. (Editor) (1975) *The Sciences, the Humanities, and the Technological Threat* London: University of London Press

Nisbet, R. (1971) *The Degradation of the Academic Dogma* London: Heinemann Educational Books

Nuffield Foundation GRIHE (1975) *Interdisciplinarity* Group for Research and Innovation in Higher Education, Nuffield Foundation, London

Percy, K. and Ramsden, P. *Independent Study. Two examples from English Higher Education* Guildford: Society for Research into Higher Education

Perry, W.G. (1970) *Forms of Intellectual and Ethical Development in the College Years: A scheme* New York: Holt, Rinehart, and Winston

Perry, W.G. (1981) Cognitive and ethical growth: the making of meaning. In Chickering, A.W. (Editor) *The Modern American College* San Francisco and London: Jossey Bass

Pippard, A.B. (1972) The structure of a morally committed university. In Lawlor, J. (Editor) *Higher Education: Patterns of Change in the 1970s* London: Routledge and Kegan Paul

Rowntree, D. (1977) *Assessing Students: How shall we know them?* New York and London: Harper and Row

The Runnymede Trust and the Radical Statistics Race Group (1980) *Britain's Black Population* London: Heinemann Educational Books

Smith, Huston (1955) *The Purpose of Higher Education* New York: Harper and Bros

Smithers, A.G. (1976) *Sandwich Courses: An Integrated Education?* Windsor: NFER

Synder, B.R. (1971) *The Hidden Curriculum* New York: Knopf

SRHE (1975) *Project Methods in Higher Education* Guildford: Society for Research into Higher Education

Swann (1968) Committee on Manpower Resources for Science and Technology, Department of Education and Science *The Flow into Employment of Scientists, Engineers and Technologists* (The Swann Report) Report of the working group on manpower for scientific growth. Cmnd.3760. London: HMSO

Willingham,, W.W. (1977) *Principles of Good Practice in Assessing Experiential Learning* Columbia, Maryland: CAEL

Zander, M. (1974) Law students and community action. In Goodlad, S. (Editor) *Education and Social Action* London: George Allen & Unwin

ACKNOWLEDGEMENTS

Dr William Birch, Director of Bristol Polytechnic, was originally to have been co-author of this chapter; what we have written owes much to his presence at our early meetings. Likewise, some of the thinking behind Propositions 1, 2 and 3 has been enriched by discussion with trustees of the Higher Education Foundation. Finally, we have benefited greatly by advice and comments from Dr William Taylor, Director of the University of London Institute of Education. While we gratefully acknowledg help from these people, we do not of course hold them responsible for what we have finally written.

4

ASSESSMENT FOR LEARNING

by Lewis Elton

INTRODUCTION
This chapter makes one recommendation, namely, *academic teachers who are concerned with student assessment and its reform should receive formal teacher training relevant to their work.*

Much has been written on the assessment of students. Most of it has assumed that assessment is necessary and even that it is a good thing, but these assumptions are rarely made explicitly. At the same time, it is generally recognized that assessment has bad side effects, but these are looked upon as if they could somehow be treated separately from the main effects of assessment which — presumably — are good. Thus Christopherson (1967, p. 87), a university teacher of wide experience, writing on examinations, has said that 'most candidates represent themselves in their papers as much less competent and well-informed than they really are.' Whenever I quote this, I get agreement to it from my academic colleagues, and yet, in spite of its great plausibility, it is an outrageous statement. I ask myself:

How does he know how competent they really are?
If he does know, is there any need to examine them?
What is it that the examination examined, if not their real competence?
Is it worth examining?
What does this process do to those who undergo it?

The purpose of this paper is to challenge and re-examine current practices. The result should be that we gain in understanding how to conduct student assessment so that as near as possible it achieves what we want it to achieve. Since our aims for assessment are many and competing, this is an optimization process in which we have to declare values and exercise judgment. In other words, it is a normal human activity. But have we always treated it as such?

The world of education is often contrasted with the 'real world', but it *is* inhabited by real people — students — who, like real people everywhere, work for rewards. These may be intrinsic or extrinsic. In the real world it has been shown (Herzberg et al. 1959) that both are needed, if people are to give of their best. Thus, very low wages discourage work, but beyond a certain limit higher wages do not produce better work. What is needed beyond that limit is an intrinsic interest in the work, personal encouragement, etc. On the other hand, these factors work only above that limit and they are ineffective if the financial reward is inadequate. In the student world, the factors of intrinsic interest and personal encouragement are much the same as anywhere, but what replaces money is marks and grades. Students rarely, if ever, put their best into work which 'does not count towards the degree' (Elton and Laurillard 1979), just as their teachers would not teach much if they were not paid. And just as their teachers, once they are paid, work very hard at what interests them and somewhat less at what does not, so will students. Only in their case the coinage consists of marks and grades. There is one further difference. In contrast with teachers, a student's 'wages' are not fixed, since some activities will yield marks much more readily than others. It is therefore not in the least surprising that the life and work of most students is strongly influenced by the assessment system which is imposed upon them.

Do I hear some of my colleagues say: 'Alright, this may be true of mediocre students, but the best transcend it'? If so, I turn on them and say: 'Did you, when you were a student?' A colleague of mine, a Fellow of the Royal Society by the time he was 30, once told me that in order to make sure of a first in the Cambridge Mathematical Tripos he had worked through every question in the examination papers of the previous ten years. He considered this necessary, although he did not think — and neither, I hope, did his tutors — that this was a good way to acquire a mathematical education.

At this point I wish to declare my own values. Students come into higher education for many reasons, but I consider it my business to help them so that they leave it with more interest in and understanding of the subject of their study than when they entered it, and with a greater ability to stand on their own feet intellectually, emotionally and morally. And because, as I have tried to indicate above, 'the spirit and style of student assessment defines the *de facto* curriculum' (Rowntree 1977), I require an assessment system to be such as to conflict as little as possible with my aims. To me, the overriding purpose of assessment is that it should encourage learning in consonance with my declared student learning aims. Even if the aims of my readers are different from mine, as they surely at least in part will be, they should share with me this overriding purpose of assessment. This is why I have called this paper 'Assessment for Learning'.

Interest in assessment and examinations has grown considerably since the Robbins Report (1963, p.189) wrote that 'We have not thought it to be within our terms of reference to enter upon the merits and demerits of the various examination systems of the universities'. The literature is now vast and I have not attempted to cover it systematically. At the same time I believe that my somewhat idiosyncratic approach to it does not misrepresent it.

PURPOSES OF ASSESSMENT

Having declared what I consider to be the overriding purpose of assessment, let me list more generally to what purposes assessment has been put. Rowntree (1977) suggests the following:

1. Selection
2. Maintaining standards
3. Motivation of students
4. Feedback to students
5. Feedback to the teacher
6. Preparation for life

To these one might add 'licence to practice a profession', although this may be considered covered by 'selection'.

These aims are very different from each other and it seems unlikely that the same form of assessment will suit all. It is noteworthy that they do not include 'testing for achievement', which is, perhaps, the most commonly-stated purpose, but this is in fact sound. Undoubtedly the process of assessment for any of the purposes listed will involve achievement testing, but it is not a purpose in itself.

Of the purposes listed, 3 and 4 help to promote learning directly and 5, one may hope, does so indirectly. To the extent that all education should aim to prepare students for the rest of their lives, Purpose 6 is also at least consonant with the overriding purpose of promoting learning, which is not to deny that an education which enables students to develop their capacities of independent thought may not prepare them for the working lives which they in fact have to lead.

Purposes 1 and 2 are very different. Selection, which includes grading since this leads to future selection, and the maintenance of standards do not in themselves encourage learning at all, although they define markers which students can only reach through appropriate learning. They are the purposes which in practice are institutionally the most important, as is immediately apparent from a scrutiny of any regulations pertaining to examinations and assessment. They also differ from the others in another way. They are concerned essentially with a product, ie the quality of students when they leave their institution, while the others are concerned with processes which the students undergo while they are at the institution. This is true even of Purpose 6, since it is the assessment process itself which constitutes a preparation for life.

We have come on to a central issue here, the importance of process in education and its comparative neglect in assessment. The reason why process is so important in education is that students mature in life and that this maturation process — which should be influenced throughout life by continuing education (see Hoggart et al. in Chapter 2 of this monograph) — is merely punctuated by the degree certification. Yet we in education often pretend that the single number which we give students at the end of their course is by itself indicative of their future development. Thus those who advocate that university selectors should consider disadvantaged pupils from inner city schools with particular 'A' level grades on a par with more fortunate pupils with slightly higher 'A' level grades are accused of 'wanting to lower standards' (Miles 1979).

We are driven to the conclusion that, if assessment is for learning, then the assessment of process must become more important than it is at present. But it goes further than that. Even for the two purposes which have least direct influence on learning, selection and the maintenance of standards, it is important to assess the process which is characterized by the learning activities of a student. Without that, selection will be less effective and it will be more difficult to maintain standards. The consequences which follow from this insistence on the assessment of process will affect much of what follows in this chapter.

Before leaving discussion of process and product, we must touch upon one other matter. The learning activities of students are strongly dependent on the learning milieu (Parlett 1977) in which they find themselves. This in turn consists very largely of a number of processes, eg a teaching process and a socialization process, to name but two. Whether students have a reasonable chance to achieve the aims which they are expected to achieve depends to a considerable degree on the extent to which these processes, which constitute the learning milieu, are consonant with the students' course aims. It is therefore necessary to evaluate them. In particular, the evaluation of teaching is the other side of the coin of which one side is the assessment of students. It is to be regretted that this was not the subject of a full paper for the SRHE Leverhulme seminar on the teaching function, although it is treated briefly and to the point by Bligh (1982). The need for it is also implicit in the strictures on present teaching practices contained in papers by Black and Sparkes in Chapter 5 of this monograph and by Gibbs (1982).

At the beginning of this section I suggested that different purposes may require different forms of assessment. However, before discussing differences we should consider what different forms of assessment ought to have in common. All assessment is a form of measurement and we therefore now turn to the properties of assessment as measurement.

ASSESSMENT AS A MEASURING INSTRUMENT

Whatever else we may expect of assessment, we would all like it to be as good a measuring instrument as we can make it. In this section we shall investigate the various properties which a good measuring instrument ought to have and how these are to be interpreted in terms of assessment. We shall find that there are four such properties and that it is in general not possible to optimize all of them at the same time. The overall optimization will therefore depend on our value judgements. The necessity for this has already been indicated in the Introduction. In much of this section we shall concentrate on formal examinations, since most research has been done on them.

Reliability

The aspect of a measuring instrument which generally springs to mind first is that we expect it to be reliable. By this we really mean two things: that it should be accurate and that if different people use it to measure the same thing, then they get the same result. Let us illustrate this with an example. If you want to measure your weight accurately, you will first weight yourself on several weighing machines. If they are accurate, then they will show the same weight. (Note, however, that they may all be distorted in the same way — an important point for examinations. In that case they lack validity, for which see below.) Secondly, you will ask several people to measure your weight, using the same machine, just in case some error is introduced through the measurement being made by different people. This may be an absurd precaution to take when you are measuring your weight, but it is normal and necessary practice in the case of scientists making delicate measurements.

There are therefore two types of reliability for a measuring instrument:

i Two supposedly equivalent instruments should give the same result when used to measure the same thing. (Test reliability)
ii Two people who used the same measuring instrument to measure the same thing, should get the same result. This includes the situation where one person measures the same thing twice. (Examiner reliability)

While in everyday physical measurements we are usually concerned with the type (i) of reliability, the opposite is the case for educational measurement. The simple reason for this is that it would normally be very difficult to set two different, but supposedly equivalent, examinations to the same candidate within a short time of each other, but it is easy to get the same examination script marked by several examiners.

The situation wherein the same script is marked by several examiners has been investigated many times, at many levels, and for many subjects. The evidence, much of which has been summarized by Cox (1967) is clear. The traditional type of examination in Britain, in which a student answers in 2—3 hours some few questions (typically 3—4 in arts subjects, rather more in the sciences) usually by choosing them from a larger number of questions offered, is worryingly unreliable. Not only do different examiners give different marks to the same candidate but they rank them in different order, and this is equally true if the same examiner re-marks a set of scripts after an interval of time.

The other kind of reliability has been investigated by McVey (1978).

For six years and on seventeen separate occasions, he set two equivalent papers within the same examination to the same students in an electrical engineering course, and these were marked by the same examiners. The correlation coefficients ranged from 0.58 to 0.87. These papers were of the problem-solving type, for which reliability of type (ii) is usually higher than for essay-type papers. The reason why the reliability of type (i) may be low for problem-solving papers is probably that problem solving depends greatly on finding a solution within a very limited time and on being familiar with the sample of basic knowledge on which the problem is based. All this introduces an element of chance, particularly for those candidates who are neither very good nor very bad. If this is so, then essay-type papers may have a higher reliability of type (i) than problem-solving papers. Unfortunately there is no evidence available to check this hypothesis, but a similar conjecture has been made by Cox (1967).

There is a third kind of reliability — test-retest reliability. If two measurements of one's weight are made a short time apart and yield different results, then one concludes that one's weight has changed. But if the same happens in an examination mark, then we are more likely to conclude that the candidate's performance is not consistent. The main reason for this difference in perception is that examinations measure a multitude of variables over most of which there is little control — eg what the candidate ate the night before — and then describe the result by a single mark.

We conclude that, for one reason or the other, traditional examinations are far from reliable. To make them more reliable the following measures can be taken, depending on which aspect of reliability we are concerned with:

a   Increase the number of questions to be answered. While this has been shown to reduce chanciness, it also rather radically alters the style of paper, since obviously the questions will have to be shorter.

b   Reduce the choice of questions and perhaps give no choice at all. If everyone has to answer the same questions, then the examination is more reliable, provided that the questions cover the whole range of work on which the students are being examined. This can be done more easily with a large number of short questions than with a small number of long questions.

c   Increase the number of markers, since averaging between markers reduces the fluctuations due to individual differences between markers. It may be noted that more rigid marking schemes, when applied to traditional examinations, have not produced significant improvement, although when combined with an increase in the number of questions on the paper, as advocated in (a) above, they have.

At this point it may be of interest to readers to carry out an experiment on one of their own examinations, ie one which they mark themselves, either by getting it marked independently by a colleague who is a fellow specialist and thus might reasonably be asked to mark that paper, or by re-marking it oneself after an interval of some weeks. Results may convince doubters. (In either case, it is essential for the two markings to be independent of each other. It is therefore important not to write on the scripts.)

Validity
At the end of the last sub-section we referred to the possibility of changing the form of an examination paper by changing the number and length of questions. Since short questions are likely to be less suitable than long ones for measuring the ability to bring together and develop different aspects of a large subject, we have thereby radically changed the nature of our measuring instrument. This illustrates a quite general rule, namely that different forms of assessment not only measure the same thing differently, but also measure different things. We say that a measuring instrument is *valid*, if it measures what it is intended to measure, and we now turn to different aspects of validity and how to ascertain the extent to which an examination is valid. In the next section we shall see that reliability and validity may not be independent of each other and that increasing the one may decrease the other.

The first requirement for validity is that an examination paper must be neither outside the curriculum with which it deals nor unduly selective within it. In other words, it must fairly reflect the curriculum. This, however, is not enough, for it is possible to ask questions of different kinds on the same curriculum content. One way of firming up on this aspect is to specify questions not only in terms of content, but also in terms of mental abilities, as for instance given by Bloom (1956). These indicate how the content is to be used, eg in terms of knowledge, comprehension, application, etc. It should be noted, however, that while Bloom is a good servant, he is a poor master. A rigid application of Bloom's taxonomy to curricular design, as demanded for instance by the Technician and Business Education Councils, can only lead to rigid and mechanical teaching.

Finally, a question must be set at the appropriate educational level which students have reached, eg first year or final year of an undergraduate course. There are therefore three specifications against which the validity of a question must be tested: content, ability and level. Whether an examination paper is valid in this sense is usually best assured by allowing an independent expert, eg a knowledgeable colleague, to check the paper against the specifications. Because this process involves the paper being 'faced' by an expert, this kind of validity is called *face validity*.

Face validity is concerned with making sure that when we measure achievement, we actually measure the achievement which we want to measure. It is therefore intrinsic to the measuring process. There are other kinds of validity which are concerned with the purposes of assessment. As we have suggested before, different purposes may call for different forms of assessment, although all must have face validity. Thus, if the purpose is selection, then the assessment must additionally have predictive validity, ie it must select the right and reject the wrong people for the task for which the selection is being made. Similarly, if the purpose is teacher feedback, the assessment must take a form which will help the teacher to improve his teaching. In contrast to face validity, validity as related to a purpose can be verified by testing the extent to which the purpose has been achieved.

Standards of Measurement
When we measure our weight in, say, kilograms, then we are really making a comparison, in that we are comparing our weight to that of a 'standard kilogram', which is a lump of metal kept at the International Bureau of Weights and Measures near Paris. There is obviously nothing quite as clear-cut in educational measurement, but it is nevertheless necessary to have standards. In this connection it is worth noting that to scientists, standards are something fixed and immutable, while educationists speak rather loosely of 'rising and falling standards' and 'keeping up standards'. What they mean by this of course is that outcomes of educational processes are rising, falling or being kept up against some standards which may or may not have been specified but are, at least in principle, constant.

In assessment we can compare the performance of a particular student either against some pre-specified performance criteria, or against the performance of a representative group of other comparable students. This enables us to establish standards, which in the first case are called *criterion-referenced* and in the second *norm-referenced*, because in the latter a student is compared to what might be called a 'normal' student. Students should at the same time be encouraged to assess their performance against their own personal progress. This method, which is called *self-referenced* is the one which experienced professional people are likely to employ more than any other when assessing their own performance, and students should be introduced to it.

A point of considerable importance in university examinations is that of the choice of the representative group in norm-referenced assessment. Rowntree (1977) suggests that it should consist of all students who in the past have taken the same examination. This would average out the inevitable fluctuations in the quality of individual year groups, which are usually not numerous enough for these fluctuations to average out within a year group. But this practice raises the difficulty of ensuring that the examination keeps to the same standard from year to year. This is overcome with large year groups — say in school leaving examinations — by assuming that the year group is of constant quality and by adjusting the examination marks accordingly if in any one year they come out too high or too low. It also, incidentally, assumes that the subject content studied for the examination is unchanged, which may not always be the case.

What happens usually in university examinations, however, is that the current year group is used to fix its own norm, although sometimes examiners use standards which they believe they carry in their minds from year to year and decide one year to give, say, more firsts, because it is a 'good year', or the opposite. Nevertheless, it has been shown that a particular university examination often maintains remarkably constant percentages for different degree classes and for failure, even when the quality of the student body, as assessed by the school leaving examination before entry, has varied substantially (Robbins 1963, pp. 190—191). This means that if students wish to make sure of, say, passing, they must do better than a certain fixed number of their fellow students. That this is likely to introduce a most unfortunate rivalry between people who ought to be friends is undeniable.

Effects of Assessment on Teaching and Learning
A further feature of examinations is their backwash effect on the teaching and learning that precedes them. The 'unfortunate rivalry' just mentioned is of course one of these effects. Ideally, a measurement should be such as not to affect what is being measured, but even in engineering that is not always possible and we may have to test the strength of an airplane wing by stressing a prototype to destruction. Testing people invariably affects them, although hopefully not to the point of destruction, and, moreover, affects them before the test takes place. To a certain extent this effect is almost bound to be bad, since the inevitable focusing of both teachers and students on to the coming examination restricts freedom and experimentation in teaching and learning. The question which we shall come back to in the next section is whether we can make this backwash at least in part beneficial.

In this section we have dealt with four specifications which a good examination — and indeed any form of measurement — ought to satisfy. Ideally, these specifications should all be satisfied. In reality some of them are likely to be no more than modestly satisfied and we may have to decide, depending on the particular purpose of an assessment and the curricular aims which it is attempting to test, on which of them we may wish to concentrate at the possible expense of the others. This will be the subject of the next section.

Our decisions should also, however, be influenced — perhaps more than they often are — by the expense of examinations and their use of resources, particularly staff and student time. The way in which limited resources are used up for examinations so that they are then not available for teaching and learning is often ignored.

One unorthodox way of saving examiners' time has been reported by Longmore and McRae (1979). It concerns the apocryphal technique of throwing a pile of examination scripts down a flight of stairs and giving the highest marks to those that travel furthest. The authors found that, provided a specified throwing technique was used, a high correlation was established with more orthodox marking procedures. Are previous uses of this technique really apocryphal or could it in the past have been used in earnest?

ASSESSMENT AND CURRICULAR AIMS

We now wish to explore how the four specifications match up to declared curricular aims. We shall concentrate first on the relative importance of reliability and validity.

It is clearly possible to make a highly reliable and totally invalid measurement by using an accurate instrument for a purpose for which it was not designed, such as measuring one's weight with a stop watch. Procedures almost as absurd *can* occur in educational measurement, when for instance an examination which is supposed to measure what has been achieved in a poetry appreciation course in fact asks questions which measure comprehension.

The reason why such situations arise is that some learning outcomes are difficult to measure reliably, and rather than measure them less reliably but more validly, they are measured less validly but more reliably. Quite generally, the less predictable a learning outcome is the less reliably can it be measured, because the more it involves the examiners' judgement. Simple recall of knowledge, like the memorizing of a poem, can be checked objectively against the original knowledge, but anything that involves the higher mental abilities — application, analysis, synthesis and evaluation, in the terms of Bloom (1956), can only be appraised in terms of the same abilities as practised subjectively by any individual examiner. It follows that the higher abilities, which are the ones which we normally wish to foster in higher education, by their very nature cannot be assessed as reliably as the lower ones. Hence there is an inescapable contradiction between high reliability and high validity in our assessment procedures.

This contradiction is re-inforced by another feature of most assessment methods, namely that they treat all candidates in the same way. This obviously makes comparability between candidates easier and so increases reliability, but it forces candidates into a uniformity which makes it difficult for them to express their creativity. Thus for assessment of creativity to have validity, it must be free of artificial constraints, such as detailed prescription of task and timespan, which in turn means that it cannot be confined within the traditional examination mould. An example of such an assessment concerns project work. (In the next section, an elaborate scheme of cross-moderation will be mentioned which attempts to achieve comparability between very different projects.) The interesting point here is that reliability is at first reduced in the interest of validity by allowing students a great deal of freedom in their choice and execution of projects, and then partially restored through procedures which do not affect the students' work. Nevertheless, overall this is a case of a reduction in reliability having to pay for an increase in validity.

The conclusion which we have reached, that reliability and validity can be traded off against each other, appears to contradict accepted wisdom in the psychometric literature which holds that it is not possible for a measurement to be valid unless it is reliable. This is correct as long as we are concerned with very high reliability, since any loss of reliability is found to lead to some loss of validity. In student assessment we are, however, inevitably dealing with much lower levels of reliability and the position here is quite different. As an analogy to student assessment we might consider the situation where we wish to measure a person's weight and have at our disposal a very unreliable weighing machine and a very accurate ruler for measuring height. The first provides a valid but unreliable measure, while the second provides a reliable measure, the validity of which is, however, in doubt because the correlation between a person's height and weight, though positive, is not high. In such circumstances, the effect on teaching and learning (here the analogy breaks down) which favours an overtly valid instrument could prove decisive.

This last point is in fact of great importance, for in stressing the need for reliability, we run the risk of testing mainly that which can be tested reliably. Not only can this have a most deleterious effect on teaching and learning, but it can actually lead to valuable areas of learning being excluded from the curriculum. This may account for the low status of aesthetic concern in, for example, literature courses and, in part at least, for the fact that our curricula in school or higher education so rarely develop spatial abilities. In the latter case, to which attention has been drawn by Patrick Nuttgens, the low cultural status of occupations associated with spatial skills is also likely to have had an effect.

Although we may wish our students to achieve high ability aims, it is entirely appropriate for a part of assessment to be at the simple knowledge level, since the possession of knowledge is necessary for its use. This is particularly so for subjects, such as the sciences, which have a complex body of knowledge which has to be assimilated. What has to be guarded against is the knowledge component in assessment becoming unreasonably large. Thus Thompson (1979) found that in most British universities more than half of the degree assessment in physics was on recall of material presented in lectures and on straightforward application of principles to problems the like of which would be familiar to candidates. Similar results in other subjects have been obtained by McGuire (1963) and by Beard and Pole (1971). A possible reason for this quite unreasonable stress on low-level abilities may lie in the knowledge explosion and the sophisticated nature of this knowledge in subjects like physics, but if this is so, then teachers must search their consciences and discover whether they really want to produce walking encyclopedias rather than active human beings. If the latter is the case, then the higher abilities must be adequately tested. Incidentally — and this is very important — if this is to be done meaningfully then the kind of knowledge to be used by candidates in displaying higher abilities under examination conditions must be such that they have had adequate opportunity during their courses to practice higher abilities on it. This could often be knowledge acquired in the earlier parts of a course, which may be substantially less sophisticated than the kind of knowledge which is tested directly.

Let us now turn to the other two specifications. There can be little doubt that the very great importance attached to final examinations is due in part to the greater ease with which it is possible to standardize them than other forms of assessment, and to then compare their standards with those obtained elsewhere. This comparison is normally made through the use of external examiners, an institution virtually unknown outside the British system of higher education and systems which derive from it.

There seems to be no research on the effectiveness of external examiners or indeed on the way in which they operate (see however Taylor 1982). Since they are nominated by the examining department, they are likely to be selected for their sympathy with that department's ethos and standards. To the best of my knowledge they are virtually never involved in curricular discussions and in fact are usually only appointed after the curriculum has been settled. Also, the subject matter of most final examinations is so extensive that no single person can be expert in all of it. My own experience was that students' answers appeared to be more original the less I knew about the subject and virtually lacking in originality where I was most expert. The suspicion that the students were equally unoriginal elsewhere and that the appearance of originality was entirely a reflection of my ignorance has since been strengthened by the work of Thompson (1979). The question whether external examiners are anything more than a cosmetic on the face of higher education must remain unanswered in the absence of research. On the other hand, it must be questioned why many criticisms of the present system are traditionally answered by reference to checks and influences of external examiners.

The most obvious and apparently inevitable effect that assessment has on teaching and learning is that a knowledge of the assessment to come concentrates teaching and learning to a greater or lesser degree on to this assessment, and that the more precisely the assessment is known, the more pronounced is this concentration. Furthermore, such concentration tends to restrict learning to the expected, while true learning should have the potential of yielding the unexpected. This is not a plea for deliberate obfuscation of learning objectives; it is a plea that such objectives should not be confined to those, the so-called behavioural ones, which can accurately pre-specify learning outcomes. Most worthwhile learning outcomes cannot be fully pre-specified and the academic was not totally misguided who, on seeing the list of objectives at the beginning of an Open University test, exclaimed: 'Surely, you don't show those to the students or they'll all pass their exams.'

It is however possible, at least in part, to counterbalance these deleterious effects by using assessment methods which reinforce good learning. To the extent that good learning almost invariably has an element of individuality in it — examples are genuine problem solving, projects, creative work — its assessment is likely to be stronger on validity than reliability. It is at this point that advantage can be taken of the educational parallel to the findings of Herzberg (1959), mentioned in the Introduction, that once students receive *some* reward, the extent of it becomes less important. Because assessment of this kind is less reliable, it may be desirable not to grade it, but to confine it to a pass/fail decision. This was done very successfully at the University of California (1966) after the riots at Berkeley which, unlike most later student protests, were actually concerned with curricular grievances.

We finally turn to the all too common situation where there is a real discrepancy between the declared aims of a curriculum and the actual aims which are being assessed and where usually the former are higher than the latter. Students then find themselves in the classical 'double bind' situation in which whatever they do is wrong. If they please their teachers and study for the declared high-level aims, they risk failing their exams; if they concentrate on the lower-level aims of the examination, they displease their teachers. (It may be noted that my colleague who later became an FRS wisely chose the latter course.) The classical study in this field is that of Snyder (1971) at the Massachusetts Institute of Technology, who showed that this discrepancy of aims can cause stress and distress to some of the most able students. The relevant British work is by Miller and Parlett (1974). They introduced the idea of 'cue-conscious' students who successfully play the system. In their study, such students were in a minority; the majority were 'cue-deaf' and tended to suffer for their naïvety.

METHODS OF ASSESSMENT

We stated earlier that it was unlikely that the different purposes of assessment and the different curricular aims it was testing could be covered by a single assessment method or indeed by the very limited range of methods normally employed. Thirteen years ago the University of Sheffield (1969) published a report on methods of assessment in which a substantial number of different methods was listed and their applicability discussed. The list, which is abstracted below, is as interesting for its inclusions as its omissions. It consisted of the following:

ASSESSMENT FOR LEARNING   119

Standard method — three-hour unseen examinations
Taking books into examinations — open-book examinations
Examinations with advance information about questions
Single question unseen paper
Access to reference material during examinations
Pre-publication of assessment marks with right of challenge
Multiple choice/objective type test
Continuous assessment
Oral examination
Thesis/dissertation

The report clearly concentrates on variants of the conditions under which the standard three-hour examination can be taken. It deals much more briefly with more radical alternatives, such as continuous assessment and oral examinations, and it does not mention short-answer questions at all. The thesis/dissertation method has become much more common in the intervening years under the title of 'project'.

Since the methods dealt with more briefly or not at all in the Sheffield report are still comparatively uncommon in higher education even today, we shall now deal with them in rather more detail.

Continuous assessment is not really a form of assessment, but a statement as to when assessment takes place. It is a term often applied to the assessment of students' work throughout their course, such as their essays, laboratory work, field work, etc. It thus relates to work which students traditionally carry out during their degree studies, so that an important question that arises is whether all of it should contribute to the final assessment or only part of it. There is evidence (Cox 1974) that it may suit some personality types better than others. If all of it contributes, students will certainly take it more seriously, but they may also feel that they are never free from the pressure of assessment. If only some of it counts towards assessment, and the rest is there for practice, then students tend to neglect the latter. One way of getting over these problems is to make every piece of course work count, but to give it two deadlines. Work handed in before the first deadline is marked, commented on and returned for improvement. The improved version is then handed in again before the second deadline and the mark on this work now counts towards the overall assessment. If students miss the first deadline, then they must still hand in their work for the second deadline, but their first attempt is now the one that counts for assessment. In this way, the choice is left to the students, as to whether they want to hand in the work in the first place for practice and comment or not. The fact that they have the opportunity of improving their first attempt also takes away a good deal of stress. A more elaborate scheme, based on the same principle, is reported by Thomas (1976).

Another way to reduce stress — at least for all but the weakest students — is to mark some course work on a pass/fail basis and not to give it a particular mark. In that way, students do not have to work their hardest for every piece of course work.

Once it has been decided that course work marks should count towards the overall assessment, it is also possible to include work, such as vacation essays, which one might not normally have expected the students to do. As was pointed out in the Introduction, students will work, and do good work, if they know that there is a tangible reward for it. One may also include oral assessment, of which more below, particularly where there is doubt about the authorship of the course work.

Course work assessment is particularly useful for assessing students' creative work which, as we have said, is very difficult to assess under controlled examination conditions. For this to be effective, the course work topic must, however, be negotiated with the student and not simply imposed by the teacher.

Under no circumstances should continuous assessment include any tests which are given for the purpose of information feedback to students. Such tests should be kept quite separate, since if they also count towards the overall assessment, they cause resentment and stress. They should normally be given with sufficient frequency (every 2—4 weeks) for students to be able to monitor their progress, but they should serve no other purpose. Under those circumstances most students welcome them. An account of students' views on continuous assessment has been given by Miller and Parlett (1974).

Oral examinations require special skills in the examiner who should receive some training in them, just as professional interviewers do. They test qualities in candidates which written examinations cannot test, such as verbal fluency, self-confidence in stressful circumstances and the ability to argue a point in a discussion. They are also notoriously unreliable and subjective and the stress which they create is often counter-productive. The main reason for this excessive stress is that students have to answer each question as it comes at them, without being able to give it more than a moment's thought. It is possible to reduce this stress by giving students some say in the questions which they are going to be asked, for example by allowing them to choose the topic for examination, either in advance or at the beginning of the oral. (In the latter case the examiner is put into the position of having to ask questions with not more than a moment's thought, which is perhaps also unnecessarily stressful.) Another possibility is for students to be presented with a list of questions at the beginning of the oral and to be given a few minutes to choose the ones on which they wish to be examined. It may be noted that the skills of oral examining are not simple and do not come naturally to most people.

A useful variant of the oral is the open-book oral. In this, a book which is known to the students in advance, and which they take into the oral, is used as the basis for the oral questioning. This method may be used with the students' own written work and is useful in checking that it is in fact their own.

It is interesting that the Sheffield report mentions multiple-choice questions, but not short-answer questions, although the latter share many of the advantageous features listed for the former, such as the possibility of a wider testing of the syllabus and of the assessment of both recall knowledge and reasoning abilities. The point to note here is that they do not share some of the most serious disadvantages of multiple choice questions, such as the considerable expense involved in their preparation and and the fact that they cannot test any divergent thinking.

It may seem paradoxical that short-answer questions often can test reasoning abilities better than long essay questions, except possibly for the very able, but this is in fact so. The explanation is simply statistical: that with a large number of short questions students can spread the risk of going wrong more evenly, while going wrong at the beginning of a long question may result in a loss of examination time of anything up to an hour. It is noticeable that for that very reason many essay and problem questions provide hints within the formulation of the question to discourage erroneous thinking. Such questions then rapidly degenerate into the category of recall and simple application.

It is possible to test a coherent body of knowledge and thought through a set of related short-answer questions and this has led to the so-called 'modified essay question' (Knox 1976). It is particularly useful in eliciting a number of responses to a case study and thus should have applicability well beyond medicine.

The remarks made above about multiple-choice questions should not be interpreted negatively. They have an important function in assessment, particularly where rapid feedback is required, where numbers are so large as to make other methods uneconomical or where it is desired to compare the results of equivalent courses in different institutions. However, they require more time and expertise in their construction than any other form of examination question and a bad multiple-choice question is probably worse than a bad question of any other kind.

We finally turn to project assessment. Project work is an attempt to introduce genuine problems into education — as near as possible as it is done in the 'real world'. In it students have to use their initiative to identify problems they wish to solve or questions they wish to explore, decide on the information, materials, equipment, etc. which they need, and how they can obtain them, use this information to plan the work, attempt to solve the problem or answer the question, and present their results coherently. In all of this, students are able to use and demonstrate much more initiative and independence than is common in other aspects of their degree work (Adderley et al. 1975).

The way to assess project work is indicated by the above list of activities which constitute the work. Thus each of the following activities ought to be assessed separately:

Identification and formulation of the problem

Information and resources needed

Planning the work

Solving the problem or answering the question

Presentation, discussion and interpretation of results

Critique of the work and recommendations for further work

The assessment methods might include written reports, seminar presentations and oral examinations. All too often the project is assessed purely on the final report. If this is done, then not surprisingly students tend to concentrate their main effort on the writing of the report and not on the work preceding it. Project assessment is inevitably individual. No two projects are alike and comparison of standards between different projects can be very difficult, although elaborate schemes of cross-marking between project supervisors can increase marker reliability. One such scheme has operated quite successfully for a number of years in the Physics Department of the University of Surrey (Jones 1981).

ASSESSMENT SCHEMES
In the last section we discussed a variety of assessment methods. We now turn to the question of how to combine these into a coherent assessment scheme. We begin with a discussion of an appropriate structure for an examination paper.

At present many examination papers at degree level consist of a number of questions, all similarly constructed, with some choice between them. Even within the compass of an examination paper this is too blunt an instrument for assessing students on their degree work. One way — and by no means the only way — to refine the instrument is by structuring it in terms of the mental abilities, such as have been provided by Bloom (1956), and which have also been used by Black and Sparkes (1982). The result might be as follows:

Knowledge
Comprehension } Multiple-choice questions (no choice)
Application } Short-answer questions (limited choice)
Analysis
Synthesis } Essay or problem questions (considerable choice)
Evaluation

The reason for the increasing choice is that the longer students are expected to take over answering a question, the more important it is to give them choice, in order to minimize the arbitrariness arising from selective preparation and defective memory.

When we turn to more comprehensive assessment schemes, which will allow us to test also for aims for which pen and paper testing is inappropriate, then we must include many of the assessment methods which we have discussed and perhaps some which we have not. This becomes particularly important when we are dealing with courses which depart from the traditional single-subject discipline orientation. Flexible courses, project-oriented courses, independent study courses, courses which involve the assessment of previous or on-going life experience, all require assessment schemes which differ substantially from those suitable for more traditional courses. Experience of such less orthodox courses in this country is very limited, although a report has recently appeared (Percy and Ramsden 1980) on the independent study courses at the University of Lancaster and North East London Polytechnic, which includes discussion of the assessment procedures used. The assessment of life experience has been an important feature of courses provided by the University Without Walls in the United States (Stetson 1979). It is also referred to in the paper by Goodlad et al. (1982). As the student body in higher education changes so that we are moving towards continuing and lifelong education, and as assessment of more diverse skills becomes more important, assessment schemes which were originally designed to suit 18-year-old school-leavers should increasingly come under scrutiny.

Another and quite different development which may force us to revise our assessment procedures is technological. As Fothergill (1982) has put it:

> 'In expressing their thoughts and ideas, students should also begin to prepare documents for their tutors in the same medley of formats that they have used to gather information. Quotations from videotape should be given on videotape alongside audio and printed forms. ... "Papers" on audio or video cassette should be as acceptable as eight sides of A4. ... Students will also begin to prepare written information by word processor, and incorporate extracts from electronic data stores. ... For the student, the ability to create in all these media becomes an essential skill that he will expect to acquire from higher educcation.'

MARKING, INTERPRETING, REPORTING

Up to this point, we have been largely concerned with the form and content of assessment. We now turn our attention more directly towards the students, who are assessed and who are affected by the assessment. When we mark, we mark students' efforts; when we shape our marking schemes, we also shape the students' study; when we publicly report our judgement, we affect and sometimes determine their lives, for good or ill. We have considerable power over our students, and we must use this power with discretion and even temper it with mercy; yet we also have a responsibility to the society for which we prepare our students. How can we maintain a balance — be fair to both students and society?

The marking of students' work involves two judgements, which should be kept quite separate. In the first, a marking scheme is decided — usually by several examiners. In the second, an individual student's work is matched against the marking scheme and a mark is awarded — this is sometimes done by one examiner and sometimes — in order to increase reliability, particularly in subjects such as literature — by more than one. If more than one examiner is involved, then it is essential that they should work independently of each other. So-called 're-marking', in which one examiner checks the marks given by another or marks a script which already contains the marks given by another examiner, does not significantly improve reliability.

How much of the judgement in marking is in the overall marking scheme and how much in the individual marking, depends on the type of question. For multiple-choice questions, all the judgement is in the marking scheme and the actual marking of scripts involves no judgement whatsoever. For essay and problem-solving questions, it is rare, although not unknown, to have a marking scheme at all. Most or all of the judgement is therefore in the individual marking of scripts. Cockburn and Ross (1978) suggest that experienced examiners do this almost entirely by 'instinct', and they are probably right.

This raises two important questions. First, how do inexperienced examiners acquire the 'instinct' which experienced examiners apparently have? Perhaps this question will become clearer if we replace the word 'instinct' by 'ability to recognize what is valuable in an essay'. There is no simple answer to this question, but a good way to acquire this ability is probably to inspect essays which have been marked by the kind of experienced examiner who writes the reasons for his decisions in the margins of the essay. (By no means all do.)

A second and quite different question is technical. How many points should a marking scale have? Experience shows that examiners rarely use more than 5—7 points when marking on an absolute scale, ie when matching each script against some standard, and that if they are given 10 points, they hardly ever use points 1, 2, 9 and 10, thus reducing the scale to about 6 points. If, on the other hand, they mark by matching scripts against each other, in order to establish a ranking, then in principle they need as many points on the scale as they have scripts, which leads to marks or grades like B- or even B- - which somehow is supposed to be different from C+ +. Such fine grading is largely spurious, in that it is difficult to get different examiners to agree on it. Fine grading can also be achieved by marking a piece of work on a number of different criteria, each on a 5—7 point scale, and then adding the marks together. The evidence is that this does not lead to more reliable marking than overall marking on a single scale (Cox 1967). Incidentally, although many examiners think that they have an absolute standard of grades in their minds, which would make their grading criterion-referenced, in practice their grading tends to be norm-referenced, ie they give roughly pre-determined proportions of each grade to any group of essay questions they are making.

The position is somewhat different for short-answer and multiple-choice questions where it is appropriate that the total assessment mark is obtained by adding together the marks obtained on a number of separate questions or parts of questions. As we stated earlier, most of the judgement is then transferred to the marking scheme, ie to the number of marks to be awarded for each question or part of a question.

The absolute marking standard which examiners tend to have in mind is usually related to their knowledge of the class of degree which is eventually associated with a particular overall percentage mark. In Britain, a common scale is as follows.

Overall percentage mark	Class of Degree
70 and over	I
60-69	II (upper)
50-59	II (lower)
40-49	III
35-39	Pass
34 and below	Fail

With this scale in mind, examiners often give only 7 or at most 8 out of 10 for a single first-class piece of work. If they do this, then it is impossible for candidates to obtain an overall first-class percentage mark unless they obtained a first-class mark on almost every single piece of work on which they were assessed. As this rarely happens it is correspondingly rare for candidates to obtain first-class degrees in assessments which are largely based on impression marking. (The same argument also leads to the conclusion, which is correct, that few fail under these circumstances.) The remedy is simple — each individual piece of work should be marked on the full scale 0—10.

The combining of marks on individual pieces of work to yield an overall mark (sometimes called 'conflating') presents considerable difficulties, since so often it involves the adding together of unlike things. (This has been discussed in very different but complementary ways by Miller and Parlett (1974) and Isaacs and Imrie (1981).)

Courses which depend a great deal on final assessment, as is the case in Britain, often leave students with comparatively little choice and flexibility in their course programmes. This is in contrast to the American pattern, where students accumulate 'credits' in individual courses, each of which is graded separately. An attempt to combine the advantages of both systems, ie to maintain an integrated course programme and yet provide the kind of flexibility inherent in the American credit scheme (Elton 1968), has by now, however, stood the test of time. In it, each part of a degree course is given a credit rating. The students then construct their degree programmes from these parts within the limits allowed. An important feature of the scheme is that different students end up with different total credit ratings for their programmes. Their final class depends on both the credit rating of their degree programme and the total assessment mark obtained; the higher the credit rating, the lower the mark required for a given degree class.

A particularly worrying feature of all assessment is that students may fail, not through faults of their own, but through faults in the system. We have previously noted evidence that examinations maintained fixed class and fail percentages, even though the quality of the intake varied. In such a situation, the percentage of failed candidates is almost predetermined and all that the assessment does is to sort out who should be the unfortunate ones to fill the fixed number of failures. (The Romans had a form of punishment, known as 'decimation', in which every tenth man in a row of men was executed. Whether you survived, depended on where the counting started, which was decided by drawing lots.) This system-induced failure rate is sometimes institutionalized by the process of mark normalization, by which the mean and spread of the mark distribution is adjusted after the marking to previously agreed norms. Under this system an unusually good group of students is pulled down and failures are artificially created, while, correspondingly, an unusually bad group gains an undeserved number of firsts.

A second artificial cause of failure is even stranger. It is quite usual, particularly in subjects where successive years build up on each other, to examine every year and not to let students proceed unless they pass. This would be justified if examinations were perfectly reliable and valid, and if students worked evenly and never improved or deteriorated. None of these conditions hold, and it has frequently been found that one year's failures succeed in the next year, if they are allowed to proceed to it. (Interestingly, this has been found to be so even in subjects where successive years build up on each other, which indicates that this build-up is actually much less important than teachers think.) If students are not allowed to proceed, then the overall failure rate builds up inexorably. There seems to be some unwritten law that on the one hand an examination is not worth setting unless some people fail, but that, on the other hand, there is something very wrong with it if too many fail. In Britain, where the school system is highly selective so that most students who manage to reach higher education *ought* to be able to obtain degrees, this means that most examinations have quite low failure rates of the order of 5—10 per cent. Hence, if a degree course examines three times (once a year for three years), the failure rate could be as high as 15—30 per cent. This may account, at least in part, for the higher failure rates in science examinations, where such annual examinations are more common than in the humanities.

Another reason why science examinations have more failures — and also, by the way, more firsts — lies in the difference between the mark distribution patterns found in science and humanities examinations. As we have already found, essay type examinations, which are common in the humanities, tend to lead to a bunching of marks in the middle with few very low or very high ones. The opposite is true for problem-solving type examinations, which are common in the sciences, where it is possible and not uncommon to obtain both zero marks and perfect marks. The fact that the sciences award far higher percentages of both failures and firsts than the humanities has been well documented and well known for at least fifteen years (since the Robbins Report, 1963), but so far nothing has been done to change the situation.

Finally, it may be noted that different policies regarding the re-taking of failed examinations can have startling consequences on overall failure rates. This can be illustrated by an example. Both engineering and medicine are professional disciplines where students should not be allowed to qualify unless they pass all their examinations. One would expect, therefore, initial failure to be high. In Britain, medicine allows liberal re-takes, but engineering does not. The figures below, which are based on data assembled by the University Grants Committee (1968), illustrate this point.

	Percentage pass		Eventual percentage academic failure
	In normal period	With extra year	
Engineering	68.4	8.0	20.1
Medicine	69.1	17.9	5.9

The figures do not add up to 100 per cent because of non-academic failures, early withdrawals, etc.

In the end, when all the assessment is finished, students are usually given a single grade or degree class. Is this really the best we can do to inform them and future employers? Rowntree (1977) provides an answer through a further question:

> 'Grades, percentages and category labels are hopelessly inadequate to convey the load of meaning that we sometimes believe we are putting into them and which other people desperately try to get out from them again. How could a single letter or number possibly tell as much, for example, as is contained in descriptive reports or profiles?'

The question of profiles has been discussed by Klug (1977). He makes it clear that he is concerned solely with an academic profile, ie a detailed report on a student's academic achievement. Such a profile could be of great value to a prospective employer, who would obtain a much more detailed — and indeed more just — picture of a graduate applying for a job, and it would supplement other evidence, such as a tutor's reference. This normally deals mainly with non-academic matters, such as personality characteristics, extra-curricular activities, etc., and it is doubtful whether anything more formal is desirable, since the methods of gathering the relevant information are themselves frequently informal and perhaps not always very reliable. Klug actually argues that it is wrong to report on such matters in *any* way.

The question of reliability also arises in connection with academic profiles. The effect of averaging a number of marks into an overall mark is likely to increase the reliability of the latter, by averaging out random fluctuations, so that the overall mark is likely to be more reliable than individual profile marks. McVey (1977) was able to throw some light on this problem by correlating marks on two equivalent papers in one subject with each other and with overall marks. He found that in nearly every instance the correlation with the overall mark was higher than that between the marks on supposedly equivalent papers. This suggests, as he says, that 'the differences between results in different subjects arise, not because of true differences in performance, but because of unreliability.'

McVey's results indicate that it may be unwise to use profile reporting for assessments in very similar subject areas, but the opposite is true of assessment in very dissimilar ones, and it is under those circumstances that the combination of marks into an overall mark is most questionable. Examples where low correlations have been found include project work and written examination papers, examinations in engineering drawing and in theoretical engineering subjects, etc. It is here that profile reporting might be most valuable.

THE MANAGEMENT OF ASSESSMENT

Throughout this paper I have drawn attention to deficiencies and malpractices common in assessment procedures in higher education. Many of these are due to ignorance, but even this excuse is invalid when we consider the management of assessment. Unfortunately there is no research whatever relevant to this subject in this country and so I have to report on my own experience over 40 years. It may not agree with everyone's experience, but I have no reason to suppose that it is untypical.

I have found it to be normal practice for examination questions to be set by individual lecturers on the courses which they themselves have taught. These courses were not documented, either in terms of a syllabus or in terms of objectives, and the only way to know their content and aims was to attend the course lectures. This the students did — indeed, it was at times the main reason why they did so. The lecturer's colleagues did not, and were thereby effectively prevented from commenting constructively on the questions. The paper committee's scrutiny of examination questions submitted to it tended therefore to be strong on the minutiae of grammar and weak on anything else. Never in my experience was a lecturer required to produce model answers or ask whether the questions had received any form of trial.

Once the paper was agreed, everything changed. Great care was taken over printing and proof reading, everything was done to ensure the confidentiality of the papers, and the formality of proceedings on the actual examination day was total. When I was an undergraduate, subfusc garments and gowns engendered — and for all I know in some universities may still engender — a sense of occasion as well as an excess of perspiration and made the experience one of an initiation rite. After the examination the scripts were sealed in heavy envelopes and carried off.

The remaining procedures were again less formal. There was little time to mark the papers and, since marks and comments were put on to the papers, a second and independent marking became impossible. The second marker's main task was therefore to check the arithmetic of the addition of marks by the first markers. (I appreciate that double marking is often done better than this, but I hope that readers will not claim virtue on this basis and ignore the rest of my strictures.) In due course, the examiners assembled as an examination board in order to settle the borderlines between classes. Since the standard error on most assessment marks exceeds the range of marks of a degree class this is a curious procedure. The board meeting did however provide an opportunity for genuinely humane treatment of hard cases. After that, the passage of the results through Faculty Board and Senate was swift to the point of carelessness.

It is possible that my experience over the years has been unfortunate and, if this is so, then I would gladly be shown to be wrong. Clearly, in institutions in which the lecturers are not also the examiners for their courses, different procedures apply and different difficulties arise.

Surveillance by the CNAA, where its writ runs, may prevent some of the abuses described. Incidentally, the question whether lecturers should or should not be examiners for their own courses has received very little discussion. Both situations create serious role conflicts, which are not easily resolved. Lecturers who are also examiners present themselves in two very different roles to their students who see the same person as both a friend and an adversary. In situations where lecturers do not examine their own courses, their friendship with their students may well be strengthened by their facing a common adversary — the examiner who, however, at other times is the lecturer's colleague. At Oxbridge, it is often a student's tutor who is his friend, as the latter is not normally the student's examiner.

The use of the word 'lecturer' so far in this section has been deliberate, for examination questions are usually set to correspond to lecture courses. In assessment schemes which use more varied forms of assessment, the teaching and assessing roles of academic staff are also more varied. There are also further malpractices to be guarded against. The first is the common practice, already referred to, of arbitrarily adding together marks obtained for very dissimilar assessments, which eventually allows examination boards to deal with the spurious accuracy of single percentage figures quoted to one decimal place (ie one part in a thousand!) The second is that students frequently do not have the complicated assessment schemes, to which they are being subjected, sufficiently explained to them. The provision of handbooks, however detailed, has frequently proved inadequate for the purpose.

On reflection, it may be that the malpractices listed in this section might also, at least in part, be due to ignorance as to how to do better. If this is so, then there might be hope that they, as well as those referred to in earlier sections, might be reduced through a programme of academic staff training and professional development, as advocated in the paper by Bligh (1982).

ASSESSMENT AND 'REAL LIFE'

Examinations, as has frequently been pointed out, are artificial situations, as are most other forms of assessment in education. What is meant by this presumably is that assessment in 'real life' takes on very different forms. And this is indeed so. There it is generally concerned with appointment to a new job or promotion in an existing job. It is accepted that this involves human judgement and that — however fallible this may be — it is preferable to the artificial reliability of formal examinations. It is hardly surprising that in these circumstances academic assessment is a poor predictor of subsequent performance in life. Thus Hudson (1960) found a poor correlation even between degree class and success in scientific research, although one could hardly think of an instance where academic training and subsequent work would correspond more closely.

The case against continuing present assessment practices is beginning to look very strong, but before turning finally to some positive suggestions as to what should perhaps be done about it, I wish to strengthen it further. It is often said that life is stressful and that the stresses engendered in students by assessment constitute a valid aspect of education as preparation for life. However, the fact that the suicide rate among university students is very much higher than for the corresponding age groups in the general population (Stengel 1964) may indicate that the stresses engendered in students are far too severe. Nicolas Malleson, who initiated student mental health services in Britain, certainly agreed with this when he once remarked that suicide is as much an occupational disease for students as silicosis is for miners.

There are other ways in which examination stress can manifest itself. Examination success can become of such importance to students that they engage in practices which are doubtfully legal or plainly illegal in order to achieve success. Such practices may include pressures on teachers by the students themselves, by their parents, or by influential persons; gifts to teachers which amount to bribery; plain cheating in examinations or the submission of course work done by others as their own. All these practices and others are known to occur in varying degrees wherever students have to pass examinations. When the competition between students is very severe, they may even resort to handicapping each other, eg a student may steal a fellow student's lecture notes, so as to prevent him from revising for an examination.

The most radical solution to the problems created by assessment is to abolish it altogether, as has indeed been advocated (Vandome et al. 1974). However, even the National Union of Students (1969) has not been in favour of total abolition, although its report came out strongly in favour of more continuous assessment. (The complaints which have arisen since then about the bad effects of this form of assessment would almost certainly have been less if the lessons of the University of California (1966) report had been heeded.) Similarly Powell and Butterworth (1972), two radical students from University College London, accept that society, as at present constituted, requires assessment, although they advocate the abolition of grading. They suggest however as an alternative — and this suggestion deserves the most serious consideration — that, when applying for a job, students should present samples of the work which they had done at university. This is of course common practice in art and architecture. Only Fawthrop (1968), one of the leaders of the student revolution of 1968, is unequivocal in his opposition:

> 'At the end of three years it should be sufficient to know that a student has indeed studied to some purpose, that of genuine learning without the "stop-go" policy of working for examinations. His degree will then reflect not his academic status, but his academic interests, his intellectual involvement, and the accomplishment of

three years of student life without a degree factory — living in an environment conducive to the real aims of education.'

Is this so very different from what the most conservative would *like* it to be?

Indeed, what sounded radical in 1968 is really not very radical at all today, and as an interim programme of reform I suggest that very serious consideration be given to the following:

1 The provision of profiles
2 The use of portfolios of work
3 The abolition of a single dimension in the degree grade

It should be noted that if the first two are accepted, the third almost follows, since the single dimension of a degree grade is in logical contradiction to the multidimensionality of profiles and portfolios. Universities could still issue degree certificates provided that a student — in Fawthrop's phrase — 'had studied to some purpose'. Whether the university which Fawthrop attended would have considered that he himself had done this is a point worth pondering on.

The fact is that the kind of changes implicit in the suggestions made above require attitudinal changes in academics and undergraduate students, which would bring their mutual relationship much closer to that which at present exists at postgraduate level at its best. There the dominant feature is one of mutual and critical help and support, leading to student autonomy in learning. That this is possible also at a lower level has recently been documented (Boud 1981). A first step towards the achievement of such autonomy lies in the use of self- and peer-assessment by students. Even this comparatively small step is one which would make most students, conditioned as they are to obey, very uncomfortable. I myself have used it in tutorials where its purpose was the improvement of essay work and not the judgement of the essays for assessment. Each student was asked to give himself a mark on his essay, put it in a sealed envelope, and then exchange essay and envelope with a fellow student. Each student then commented on and marked his fellow student's essay and the two finally got together to discuss the comments and their respective marks for each essay. Disagreements could be brought for further discussion to me as teacher. There is no doubt that the students found the procedure both difficult and strange, which is not surprising since it puts students into very unfamiliar situations. Experience with it certainly indicated that it would be unwise to involve students in judgemental assessment until they had become familiar with and had learnt the skills of assessment through self- and peer-assessment for improvement.

CONCLUSION

This paper has attempted to demonstrate and document the deficiencies of our present assessment methods and the deleterious effect that they have on worthwhile teaching and learning. In the last section I then related assessment to what is called 'real life', where formal assessment is notable by its absence. This led me to ask whether it should be equally absent in education, and I then progressively stepped back from this very radical solution to a point where I could make contact with present practice. What I wish to stress is that every one of the measures which I have suggested as appropriate to take us from the present to an improved future has been tried successfully somewhere; what is necessary is to co-ordinate them and adapt them to circumstances in which they have not previously been tried. To do this effectively is not however easy. It requires an understanding of the process of teaching and learning with particular reference to the subject and discipline of study. In other words, it requires at least those teachers in higher education who are particularly concerned with student assessment to be much more familiar with the pedagogic side than they normally are, or could be expected to be without some formal training. I therefore close this chapter by repeating the one firm recommendation.

Recommendation 1
Academic teachers who are concerned with student assessment and its reform should receive formal teacher training relevant to their work.

ACKNOWLEDGEMENT

My thanks are due to Donald Bligh for most helpful comments on the first draft of this paper.

REFERENCES

Adderley, K. et al. (1975) *Project Methods in Higher Education* Guildford: Society for Research into Higher Education

Beard, R.M. and Pole, K. (1971) The content and purpose of biochemistry examinations *British Journal of Medical Education* 5, 13-21

Black, P.J. and Sparkes J.J. (1982) Teaching and learning. Chapter 5 of this volume

Bligh, D.A. (1982) Is professional development possible? Chapter 2 in Bligh, D.A. (Editor) (1982) *Accountability or Freedom for Teachers?* Guildford: Society for Research into Higher Education

Bloom, B.S. et al. (1956) *Taxonomy of Educational Objectives* London: Longmans

Boud, D. (Editor) (1981) *Developing Student Autonomy in Learning* London: Kogan Page

Christopherson, D.G. (1967) *The Engineer in the University* London: English University Press

Cockburn, B. and Ross, A. (1978) *Teaching in Higher Education. No. 8:*

Essays University of Lancaster

Cox, R.J. (1967) Examinations and higher education: a survey of the literature *Universities Quarterly* 21, 292-340

Cox, R.J. (1974) *Students and Student Assessment: A study of different perceptions and patterns of response to varied forms of assessment in the University of Essex* PhD thesis, University of Essex (unpublished)

Elton, L.R.B. (1968) The assessment of students — a new approach *Universities Quarterly* 22, 291—301

Elton, L.R.B. and Laurillard, D.M. (1979) Trends in research in student learning *Studies in Higher Education* 4, 87—102

Fawthrop, T. (1968) *Education or Examination* London: Radical Student Alliance

Fothergill, R. (1982) *New Technology and the Teaching/Learning Function* Paper presented to the SRHE Leverhulme seminar on the teaching function, Bristol Polytechnic

Gibbs, G. (1982) *The Teaching Function or the Learning Function* Paper presented to the SRHE Leverhulme seminar on the teaching function, Bristol Polytechnic

Goodlad, S. and Pippard, B. with Bligh, D.A. (1982) The curriculum of higher education. Chapter 3 of this volume.

Herzberg, F., Mausner, B. and Snyderman, B. (1959) *The Motivation to Work* London: Staple Press

Hoggart, R., Stephens, M., Smethurst, R., Taylor, J. (1982) Continuing education within universities and polytechnics. Chapter 2 of this volume

Hudson, L. (1960) Degree class and attainment in scientific research *British Journal of Psychology* 51, 67—73

Isaacs, G. and Imrie, B.W. (1981) A case for professional judgement when combining marks *Assessment and Evaluation in Higher Education* 6, 3—25

Jones, M.C. (1981) *Notes for Guidance on Project Report and Assessment* University of Surrey, unpublished

Klug, B. (1977) *The Grading Game* London: National Union of Students

Knox, J.D.E. (1976) *The Modified Essay Question* Medical Education Booklet No 3. Dundee: Association for the Study of Medical Education

Longmore, R.B. and McRae, D.A. (1979) Random assessment by projected examination scripts: a new look at examination marking *British Medical Journal* 22—29.12.1979, pp.1640—1641

McGuire, C.H. (1963) A process approach to the construction and analysis of medical examinations *Journal of Medical Education* 38, 556

McVey, P.J. (1977) Subject profiles viewed in the light of reliability *Assessment in Higher Education* 2, 181—190

McVey P.J. (1978) A comparison of reliability: objective and conventional examinations in electronic engineering *International Journal of Electrical Engineering Education* 15, 109—114

Miles, H.B. (1979) *Some Factors Affecting Attainment at 18+ A Study of Examination Performance in British Schools* Pergamon

Miller, C.M.L. and Parlett, M.R. (1974) *Up to the Mark:* London: Society for Research into Higher Education

National Union of Students (1969) *Executive Report on Examinations* London

Parlett, M.R. (1977) The department as a learning milieu *Studies in Higher Education* 2, 173—181

Percy, K. and Ramsden,, P. (1980) *Independent Study* Guildford: Society for Research into Higher Education

Powell, A. and Butterworth, B. (ca 1972) *Marked for Life* Published privately

Robbins Report (1963) *Higher Education* Cmnd. 2154. London: HMSO

Rowntree, D. (1977) *Assessing Students: how shall we know them?* London: Harper and Row

Snyder, B.R. (1971) *The Hidden Curriculum* New York: Knopf

Stengel, E. (1964) *Suicide and Attempted Suicide* Penguin Books

Stetson, K.W. (1979) *University without Walls* Chicago: Interversitas

Taylor, L. (1982) Laurie Taylor devoted his column in the *Times Higher Education Supplement* of 19 March 1982 to the issue of external examiners

Thomas, R.H. (1976) The necessity of examinations and their reform *Studies in Higher Education* 1, 23—29

Thompson, N. (1979) The assessment of candidates for degrees in physics *Studies in Higher Education* 4, 169—180

University Grants Committee (1968) *Enquiry into Student Progress* London: HMSO

University of California (1966) *Education at Berkeley* Report of the Select Committee on Education, Berkeley; p.99—100

University of Sheffield (1969) *Report of the Working Party on the Assessment of Students* Unpublished

Vandome et al. (1974) Why assessment? In Upton, L. (Editor) *An Examination of Assessment* London: NUS publications; pp.53—59

TEACHING AND LEARNING

by Paul Black and John Sparkes

INTRODUCTION

Summary of the Arguments
The main arguments of this chapter can be summed up in the list of propositions set out below.

1. *Staff ought to be more aware of the effect of their teaching on their students; staff ought to be more sensitive to the factors which inhibit personal relationships with their students.*
2. *For most educational aims appropriate to higher education, students need personal feedback if they are to learn successfully. High priority ought to be given to providing such feedback where it is needed, by any of a variety of methods.*
3. *Staff should have a clear, agreed set of aims for their teaching and for student learning, which are shared with and explained to students, which are reflected in the planning of courses and which are matched to the teaching methods used.*
4. *In the design of teaching, the central focus should be to stimulate, guide and support the individual student in his or her struggle to learn; from this it follows that*
   a *Teachers should be aware of the strengths and limitations of different teaching methods, in relation to different educational aims. Even good lectures can only make a limited contribution, and where they are bad they must be changed or abandoned.*
   b *Students must be assisted to guide and assess themselves by materials for individualized learning and for self-assessment.*
   c *Projects, because of their ability to integrate different educational aims, and the strong motivation to learn which they provide, should be widely used where they are appropriate.*
5. *Students should achieve a clear understanding of their aims, of the way in which each course is designed to meet these aims, and of the role of different teaching methods within the design. Such understanding should lead them to take more responsibility for their own learning and to take part in constructive criticism of courses.*
6. *Staff should commit themselves to becoming professional teachers; this involves, inter alia, the need to maintain minimum acceptable standards in teaching.*

7 *Professionalism in teaching in higher education implies*
  a *More public exposure and discussion of teaching performance, course design and teaching materials.*
  b *High scholarly status given within a discipline to the design and delivery of good teaching in that discipline.*
  c *Use of appropriate models and strategies for the 'engineering' of teaching.*
8 *The main responsibility for improving teaching within a discipline must belong to scholars in that discipline; experts in teaching methods can support and advise, whilst those equipped for research into teaching and learning should devote some of their resources to research commissioned by teachers.*
9 *Staff ought to know about the wide range of teaching methods now available; they should be able to select those methods which are most effective for the aims and contexts of the learning. In particular most staff need to learn more about the professional skills needed for independent study and distance-learning methods.*
10 *Institutions should accept the need to define professional standards in teaching and should develop structures to stimulate and support staff in meeting such standards. This means that they must actively support the professional development of staff as teachers, including the learning of new skills and the development and use of methods to assess teaching work.*
11 *Institutional systems for consultation, for making decisions and for delegating authority should be constant with the needs and rights of staff in teaching, whether as individuals or as course teams.*
12 *Staff should be aware of the relative costs per student hour of various methods, should bear these in mind in designing courses and should pursue collaboration with other institutions for the sharing of resources and materials wherever possible.*
13 *Innovations in teaching need particular support and protection if they are to develop their full potential and if the staff involved are to have a fair reward for the risks that they take.*

Main Themes
One of our main underlying themes is our belief that it is both possible and desirable to achieve a much higher standard in teaching in higher education in this country. This is not to say that teaching is generally poor or that standards achieved are lower than those in other countries. Indeed, there are numerous instances of very good teaching and our systems do not suffer from some of the inherent weaknesses which afflict teaching in the rest of the world. However, instances of unsatisfactory or really poor teaching, which is often repeated over years without correction, are sufficiently common to cause concern, and we not only believe that where this occurs it is often too readily accepted but also that staff

and students could generally achieve much more if teaching and learning were taken more seriously.

A second theme is that in considering teaching and learning, the personal attitudes and responses of those involved are of first importance. Thus we try here to highlight the personal impact of teaching upon students and to draw attention to the personal re-orientations needed if the situation is to improve.

A third theme is that in order to design teaching systems more effectively, some simple models have to be adopted so that plans have a coherent basis. Those offered are deliberately simple so that they emphasize key features of the teaching and learning process, and so help with the 'engineering' of teaching. Although they can certainly be refined to make them more accurate, they are found, in this form, to be very helpful in the design of teaching and learning systems.

Background to the Arguments

This chapter focuses on the notion of higher education as a system. That is, it stresses the fact that there are many aspects to the achievement of success in teaching and learning at the tertiary level and that they are all likely to interact at certain times. Even although it is possible to identify several fairly distinct sub-systems, such as open-learning systems, distance-teaching institutions and conventional campus universities, interactions still occur at many levels. Equally the ingredients of successful teaching and learning involve not only an understanding of educational aims and methods and an appreciation of the expectations and needs of both students and staff, but also the effective management of the various kinds of institution and their costs. The task here, therefore, is to present both a picture and an analysis of the teaching and learning functions which illuminate some of the key features of the system without diminishing the significance of their interdependences.

Thus, for example, we begin by focusing on the notion of a campus based institution of higher education as a community. Since the aim of this community is teaching, learning and research, it ought to function as a community within and through those activities. This is not to deny the importance of social leisure or other broader activities, only to assert that the way people *work* together matters centrally.

There is possible confusion here about means and ends. As a means, one might regard the establishment of the right relationship and mutual involvement of students and staff from several points of view, all to be judged from a criterion of effective learning. This is important enough: there is enough prima facie evidence that the way students feel about their teachers affects their work, and similarly that a teacher's contact and involvement with students affects his capacity to teach well, and to learn how to improve.

However, a higher education course is also a part of a student's life,

TEACHING AND LEARNING 139

not merely a preparation for a later stage, and the institution is sometimes the whole of the academic's working life. So it ought to be a place in which it is worthwhile to live and work. That is to say, the institutions should be concerned with the mutual relationships of the members. More ambitiously, they should be trying to set a standard of how people should relate and how a structure should serve those relationships, as one element of a free society.

The above points do not do justice to the importance and subtlety of the issues. Members of any organization adopt roles in an attempt to achieve equilibrium between their perception of its demands and constraints, and their own aims, beliefs and fears. The perceptions of an organization are more personal, and differ far more widely between different individuals, than most of us recognize, and yet these perceptions, being the maps by which individuals set their various courses, have very strong effects on the way they decide and act. Conversely, the structure and effects of an organization on its members is affected by each of them, often in ways they do not understand.

All this is to argue that the human dynamics of an institution cannot be ignored in discussion of effective teaching and learning. This is just as true, and perhaps more difficult to understand, in distance-teaching institutions — including, for example, educational TV — as it is in face-to-face ones.

Equally, the manner in which new skills, knowledge, understanding or attitudes are acquired by students depends not only on how they are taught, on the methods used, but also on the learning processes involved and on how they relate to such differing educational aims. But even if all these aspects of the process were well understood and under good control, they could fail if the learning *milieu* were not satisfactory.

The discussion below sets out an agenda which concentrates, in separate sections, first on students and then on academic staff. A final section discusses some aspects of institutions as educational systems, and pays some attention to such issues as power and authority, costing and the conditions for effecting change.

However, within these sections the paper interleaves the evidence presented with simple models and analyses of the teaching and learning processes, against which the evidence can be understood. Thus the discussion takes place at two levels. Throughout the paper a number of recommendations for action of one kind or another are stated. Their purpose is to bring about an improvement in teaching and learning in higher education.

Finally, in this introduction it should also be pointed out that although much of the discussion is applicable to higher education in general, there is a bias towards the problems of education in science, since it is from this area that most of the evidence has been obtained.

STUDENTS

Proposition 1. Evidence
Staff ought to be more aware of the effects of their teaching on their students; staff ought to be more sensitive to the factors which inhibit personal relationships with their students.

Most staff have their own working model of what students are like and of what it is like to be a student. These perceptions are often misleading in ways that matter: in particular they can be inaccurate in underestimating the intellectual distance between staff and student, they can be completely wrong in assumptions adopted about the student's perceptions of the institution and of his role within it, and they can be anaesthetic in playing down the personal impact on the student of weakness in the teaching system. The perceptions are often wrong not merely from lack of better information, but because they are themselves a protective reaction for the lecturer.

It might be helpful to start again — to imagine the students as extra-terrestrial aliens and to study new information in order to build a new model.

To illustrate what this might involve, we would like to quote here some of the results of the Higher Education Learning Project in Physics (Ogborn 1977a, 1977b; Bliss and Ogborn 1977; Bridge and Elton 1977). In that project a group were trying to find ways to help improve the contact between the university teacher and the learner. One way was to interview students at length, choosing them from about ten different universities and collecting from them, in a fairly open and free way, their stories about incidents in learning which seemed significant to them. They were asked to tell good and bad stories, one of each, so that a total of 300 stories were collected, almost equally divided between the good and the bad. They were given a free choice of topics and the most popular single area was that of lectures, which obviously seem to be the most important aspect of learning for many of the students.

A useful way of making the evidence both authentic and incisive is to consider some extracts taken from the transcripts of these interviews. So here are students talking about lectures.

1   'Well the lecturer gave the impression of informality, you know and sort of was easy all the way through the problem. If anyone felt that either he was going too fast or too slow or they couldn't understand him, they wanted him to rewrite it, if they couldn't read it then he would do it. I think you could say it was stimulating, you were interested in learning. It wasn't actually you know, sort of, get into the lecture and somebody gets up and dictates how they want it done but you had the feeling you were part of it, you felt you were contributing towards the lecture.'

2 'I think my general feeling when I went to the lecture courses was just a complete blank. There is nothing that I could, I mean, it wasn't that I was really scared of the subject — I wasn't really but oh God this is far beyond me — I just couldn't do it. I went there and after ten minutes, sometimes before ten minutes, I said I would do something, I would try to understand, I would try to think what he was doing but after ten minutes I just became lost in a jungle of symbols. There was nothing I could identify I just couldn't take anything in at all. I did feel scared when I walked out, a few times because I thought you know maybe I shouldn't have come to university, maybe I haven't got the intelligence for going it you know.'
3 'You get the feeling that if everybody walked out from the lecture he wouldn't notice you know. If you walked out or not instead of real life students we had cardboard cut-outs he would still carry on talking and writing on the board.'
4 'One particular incident, when I felt bad in a lecture was when one of the lecturers hadn't been doing too well was asked a question, and he couldn't explain it. Well he knew but he couldn't communicate and the guy sort of kept at him and in the end the lecturer sort of said "Well I know even if you don't" sort of thing. Everyone felt depressed after that.'
5 'Dr X's courses was something he does research into it and his lectures are really interesting, he is really interested in the subject and it really came over well to you that he was trying to explain — he is just so enthusiastic about it, he will tell you a bit about what his own work is connected with the subject so it is not just theory churned out sort of meaningless, you know, it really makes sense to you. Well I suppose it is just that I want to learn more about it, and maybe understand it properly.'
6 'It was pretty useless I can't describe it. You go into your lecture at say ten o'clock and you sit down, at five past ten you are writing away, at ten past ten it feels like an hour you have been there — you are still writing. Half-past ten you feel you have been there for three weeks. I think you are consciously looking at your watch and saying we will be finished in 20 minutes, finished in 19 minutes, 18 minutes 25 seconds, just finish, finish, finish for God's sake shut up and go.'

Bad stories predominated for lectures: since the sample as a whole was balanced they were compensated by an excess of good stories in some other areas.

The physics students in the study chose to discuss lectures for about 50 per cent of their interview 'stories'. Tutorials, by contrast, were the subject of only 10 per cent of the 'stories'. It was depressing to find that this one personal part of science teaching was of such low significance.

The tutorial stories were equally divided between good and bad. About half the good and almost all of the bad were about tutors' ability or inability to explain things. The issue in tutorials for a student is whether or not the explanation works for him personally. Thus:

7 'He was really helpful, because if you didn't understand a part of the course, he would go through it even three or four times if necessary. I think tutorials are the most important part of the course, because you do actually talk to a doctor close to and get something from him — and he is giving it only to you, he is able to concentrate on what you actually want.'

The main feelings in such cases were satisfaction and security:

8 'It was just a sort of general elation at the fact that I had learned something. That made me happy.'
9 'Suddenly you understand it, and you think "Ah, I understand and I don't have to worry now." ... It's a relief that you can understand it now whereas you didn't before. It eases your burden of worries.'

Such outcomes were then a spur to further work:

10 'If you find you can understand that far, it urges you on to have a stab at the other bits.'

However, when the tutors' attempts to explain were a failure, then a characteristic reaction was of annoyance, and this annoyance was partly directed at the tutor. Another common effect of failure to learn was that the student felt that the tutor was not trying, or was not able, to help him at his level. The reactions in the following extract, of not bothering with the subject and of loss of liking and respect for the tutor (as opposed to being angry) were also quite common.

11 'He'd say, "Any problems?", and we would maybe bring up one or two minor problems, but he never really got to us in a sense, and we never brought him anything significant. ... Once we went to see him, and he got some textbooks out and we went through them on the blackboard, until we discovered that he'd confused himself completely. Just didn't know anything about it. (So) I didn't bother revising it ... and there was no respect for him.'

Loss of respect also took more amusing forms:

12 'I would simply prefer that if you have got problems to go and see the bloke who is doing the lectures, but they always advise you to go and see your tutor first. They (university) obviously haven't

realized that the tutor can't be expected to know everything. So it means harder work for us, trying to find something for him to do in 50 minutes to stop him setting us work that we don't want to do.'

Many students' accounts of tutorials focused more directly on the interpersonal aspect. The following extract contrasts well two different types of experience.

13 'You felt that this bloke cared about you. ... I always felt sad when it was over — if the conversation gets going an hour can just fly by. You felt he had put the effort in. Physics got taught there as well, but it wasn't "Come in — let's do some physics", but, "Come in — have you got anything to talk about?" Whereas with some tutorials it is, "Hello — come in — now what about Fermi energy — who knows anything about that?", and waiting for some brave guy to open his mouth and be ridiculed. And it was reassuring to know there was somebody with a bit more knowledge of life that you could go and see — this bloke made it friendly, you know, at least he said you can rely on me.'

The feelings of threat that tutorials can generate are striking. The following illustrates these feelings:

14 'He treats subjects reasonably simply, and he makes us work in his tutorials, but you don't mind working for him. There are other people who stand at the front with a piece of chalk and you think "in about ten minutes he's going to hand that (chalk) to me and he's going to tell me to do something on the board and I am not going to be able to do it." So you don't have the right attitude in most tutorials, but with Dr... it's not true. I don't know what it is, whether it's his personality or the way he treats tutorials, but I don't mind saying something and being wrong in his tutorials, but I do in others.'

15 'I can't think. ... I know I was absolutely petrified of tutors. Four of us used to go along to the tutorials and I never used to say a thing. Or if I did it was something very small. The more I thought I must say something the more I didn't and just closed up like a clam. I know once I was on the edge of being reduced to tears, I can't remember what it was, but I know I was so clamped up. I think the tutor was in an ill humour. I forget and he said something like 'oh rubbish' or something like that and I'd said something and it was sat on. At first I was upset and then afterwards I was angry because he ought to have realized. ... I think he ought to have realized that I was making a contribution.'

Much of what students said reflected how well or badly a tutor had dealt with their nervousness. Another common theme reflected on the lack of real communication between tutors and students. Often this goes with the idea of using a tutorial for remedial purposes but with a failure on both sides to do any preparation work for the tutorial.

16 'You'd come in and he'd say 'any questions?'. Oh. Then he'd I don't know, he'd sort of pick up the last lecture notes from somewhere and sort of start asking questions on them, explaining bits that weren't even difficult. If you asked him a question, he'd wander on and on and on and on, you know, he'd go past the question and then go on and on. The whole thing was a bore.'

The difficulties and successes that these pieces of evidence reveal seem to arise from a variety of causes; some were concerned with personal matters such as the fear of making a fool of oneself or the nature of the relationship between student and tutor, and others were concerned with the actual teaching activities themselves. Lectures and tutorials in some cases come in for a good deal of criticism. The areas in which good stories were in excess were the areas in which students were talking about projects, about essays, and about other types of work in which there was some degree of personal responsibility and involvement.

It is hard to know how to make sense of evidence of this kind. The matters involved are complex, yet action to improve requires that some simple models be adopted as a guide. Two such models are adopted below and subsequent discussion first shows how these help to understand the problems exposed above, and then returns to a broader consideration of the development of students.

Proposition 2. The Feedback Model of the Learning Process
For most educational aims appropriate to higher education, students need personal feedback if they are to learn successfully. High priority ought to be given to providing such feedback where it is needed, by any of a variety of methods.

We have called the descriptions given under Propositions 2 and 3 'models' because each gives a simplified view of different, but interrelated aspects of a complex situation. It is beside the point to argue that they are incomplete since they are intended to act as guides to the practice or 'engineering' of teaching. (In much the same way engineers design most of their technology using Newtonian mechanics even though it is known to be incomplete as compared with Relativity.) The purpose of these models, therefore, is to emphasize key features of the teaching and learning processes, to highlight distinctions that are important from a teaching point of view and facilitate the matching of teaching and learning methods to both the needs of students and the subject matter they are trying to learn. They represent little more than an explicit statement of what is fairly well known by most experienced teachers, but which is also forgotten when one is faced with the kind of evidence presented earlier. It is a common experience that teaching and learning are improved when errors and inadequacies are diagnosed and, preferably, dealt with in some way. Equally, both processes benefit when good performance is encouraged. So the importance of such feedback processes in education can hardly be a matter of argument. The following remarks merely encapsulate this idea in a formal model. Figure 5.1 represents a feedback model of the educational process. It exemplifies Pask's 'conversational' model (1976) since it illustrates that learning is achieved by a *continuous iteration between absorbing new information, trying to use it, and checking whether it was correctly used.* In other words, concepts are recycled by the learner and gradually acquire sufficient richness of meaning for them in the end to be used with confidence to express the learner's own ideas. Such a process applies to learning a language and the meaning of words, to acquiring skills as well as to learning concepts and ideas.

Referring to Figure 5.1, the output of the system is (intended to be) educated students. If the forward path were faultless, and if all students could learn immediately, the output could be achieved without feedback playing a part. In practice, however, the forward path (eg written teaching texts, lectures, TV programmes, etc.) is rarely wholly successful educationally, students do not live up to expectation, and they need help. They may also lose confidence and choose to give up or stop trying very hard. So it is necessary to include feedback in the system in order to provide encouragement to study and to correct any errors that occur, whether in the performance of teacher or of students, and so to provide 'conversational' recycling of ideas.

The model applies to situations in which the teachers prescribe the course of study as well as to those in which individualized learning methods dominate. In one case the 'energy' driving the feedback system comes from the teachers, in the other it comes from the students. For most purposes contributions from both participants are desirable.

Several kinds of feedback are possible. They have different characteristics and serve different functions. In descending order of response time these are:

a   *The statistical feedback* (shown dashed), obtained from large surveys of student response, indicates whether the forward path is appropriate for the chosen target student population. The time period within which changes to the forward path can be made in response to this kind of feedback is so long that it can normally only affect the next, or next-but-one, cohort of students. It does not, therefore, play any part in the conversational learning process. It is useful only as a means of correcting gross errors in the forward

FIGURE 5.1
A feedback model of the teaching process

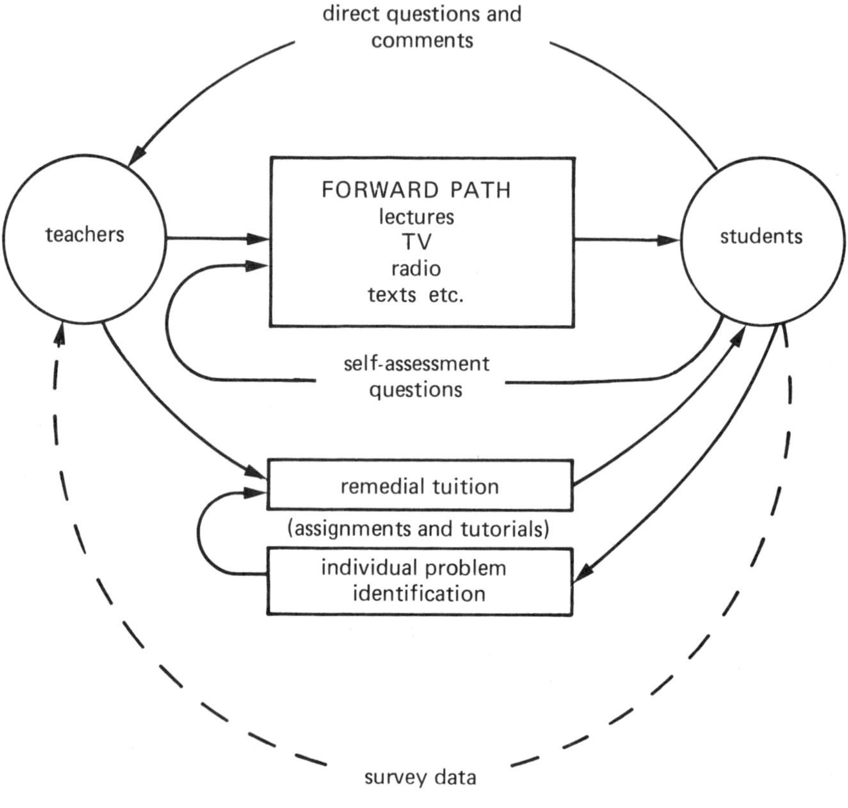
direct questions and comments
teachers
FORWARD PATH
lectures
TV
radio
texts etc.
students
self-assessment questions
remedial tuition
(assignments and tutorials)
individual problem identification
survey data

A feedback model of the teaching process. Students can receive or request help from their teachers (or elsewhere) in a more or less continuous interaction. Differing educational aims require different degrees of interaction between teachers and learners. In general, the learning of intellectual skills requires the most interaction; the learning of facts requires the least.

path, but whilst it indicates that the outcome is unsatisfactory, it cannot show directly how matters could be improved.

b *Assignments* have a response time of a few weeks and provide specific help to each individual student. To obtain the best educational effects from assignments tutors should give helpful comments on scripts. Computer-marked assignments (CMAs) linked to a pre-programmed word processor can provide similar help with certain kinds of topics. Assignments can fulfil different roles: for example (i) assess a student's performance (and award marks), (ii) correct errors by giving correct or model answers, and (iii) encourage further work on the problem so that students will arrive at better performances by their own efforts. As far as effective learning is concerned the last role is generally the most important since it helps to sustain a student's involvement.

c *Tutorials, telephone conferencing and 'self-help' groups* provide immediate feedback and true 'conversational' learning. A useful distinction can however be drawn between 'individual-problem-identification' and 'remedial tuition' as shown in the diagram. The tutor has to find if students have 'any problems' and then remedy them as best he can. Computer methods, however, can be used for individual-problem-identification, and various alternative methods can be specified for the provision of remedial teaching (eg computer-exercises, dial access by telephone, telephone calls, specified face-to-face tutorials, audio-vision, teaching packages, Cyclops tapes, etc.) Combining both aspects (problem identification as well as remedial tuition) in face-to-face tutorials is rarely as successful as one would wish (see later comments).

d *Self-assessment questions* in teaching texts, or short quizzes or tests in lectures or tutorials provide the simplest stimulant to internal conversational learning.

The small group teaching of the kind that occurs in many sixth forms, for example, in schools provides one of the richest teaching and learning environments for various reasons. It includes much personal and intellectual interaction: it goes at a pace which is regulated by this interaction; it occurs sufficiently frequently for teachers and pupils to get to know one another well and they can become mutually very supportive and rewarding. In other words, the feedback process can operate successfully at a variety of levels.

With this as a model for at least some kinds of teaching and learning it is possible to suggest how it is that students have not, on the whole, responded favourably to some kinds of lectures and tutorials.

The lecture is often criticized because it does not teach well; but we can now see that it is an incomplete teaching and learning system. Interaction, either at a personal level or at an academic level is cut to a minimum, and indeed much of the onus for learning is thrown upon the students, through private study of books or lecture notes, through discussion with fellow students or tutors and through exercises, either self-assessed or submitted to tutors. Few experienced lecturers expect their students to have *learnt* what has been covered in the lecture by the end of the lecture: the main aim has been to provide an explanatory account of what has to be learnt and/or understood.

This lack of interaction between students and teacher has various consequences. On the positive side it does, of course, tend to force (some) students to study on their own and not be 'spoon-fed' or 'crammed' as sometimes occurs at schools. On the other hand, however, failure to close the feedback loop allows a lecturer to go much faster and only leave time for rapid note-taking: to be as obscure as he wishes without the corrective action of feedback. Such tactics can so inhibit personal communication that only the brave extroverts interrupt the flow.

As we shall see in a moment, not all aspects of learning require feedback (though perhaps all aspects of teaching do). So lectures have a valuable part to play, but not, in general, in the teaching of difficult concepts.

Similar, though different, comments can be made about small group classes. They are an almost ideal teaching forum except for their most widely used activity — remedial teaching on a topic taught elsewhere by some other teacher (eg in a lecture or film or TV programme or teaching text). 'Individual-problem-identification' cannot be achieved easily in a group — even in a small group, and 'remedial tuition' is always likely to interest only a minority of the group. However, in many school sixth forms, the group's work is the primary teaching 'medium' as well as means for immediate and effective feedback and where groups can also meet frequently they are very successful. Much smaller contact hours and the aim of encouraging private study tend to rule out such uses of small classes for such purposes in universities though it might well be sensible to use them for the teaching of specific difficult concepts as well as for exercising certain intellectual skills.

So the main thing that is wrong with lectures and seminars is that they are used by staff, and expected by students, to fulfil a role to which they are ill-suited. No doubt a good deal can be achieved by teaching teachers how best to use lectures and tutorials, but frequent attempts in the past to achieve such lecturer-training have not been very successful, because of the inherent drawbacks of these methods, as already explained. The lecturer-education that would be worthwhile would be (a) giving clear guidance as to the roles that lectures and small groups can serve well, so that they are not used inappropriately and (b) explaining the capabilities of other teaching methods such as film, TV, audio-tape, tutor-texts, computers, etc., by means of which some of the deficiences of face-to-face teaching can be made good.

In addition it should be emphasized that the importance of feedback in teaching varies according to both student characteristics and student educational aims. It is, for example, more important in the learning of skills than in the learning of factual knowledge. These distinctions form the subject matter of our second model.

Proposition 3. A Model for Distinguishing between Educational Aims
Staff should have a clear, agreed set of aims for their teaching and for student learning, which are shared with and explained to students, which are reflected in the planning of courses and which are matched to the teaching methods used.

It is well known that there are different *kinds* of learning. For example, the learning of skills is a very different activity from the acquiring of knowledge or from embracing a belief in, say, religion or Marxism or apartheid. Yet it is not always apparent that the teaching and learning methods used to achieve these different educational aims take full account of such differences.

A key step in identifying which teaching methods are most effective in achieving particular aims, and which are less effective, is the establishment of a few easily distinguished categories of educational aims. Once again we are concerned with the establishment of a 'model' which serves only to exhibit some broad categories that can readily be recognized, even although they may to some extent overlap and interrelate. (In much the same way we distinguish between the seven colours of the rainbow even although there are no clear dividing lines in the continuous spectrum). The purpose of the categorization is to help with the choice of teaching methods, so the model must be shaped to some extent so that it maps onto the characteristics of different teaching methods. As with all models this simplified description of reality serves to fulfil a particular purpose, which is to help to identify the kinds of educational aim for which various methods, such as lectures or audio-tapes or TV, are appropriate.

The following set of eight categories, which borrow a little from Bloom's taxonomy, seems to meet these requirements (see p. 150).

These eight categories can be further explained and illustrated as follows.

The Affective Domain The affective domain is concerned with values, beliefs, attitudes and habits. Such factors tend to be deeply ingrained and firmly defended or justified. Habitual behaviour, whether it is resistance to change, intolerance or carelessness, is as difficult to change as one's beliefs in religion, or science, or apartheid. All the same they do sometimes change, usually as a result of social pressures of one kind or another, although an unforgettable novel, TV programme or experience can sometimes penetrate deeply enough.

The TV programme 'The Chips are Down' changed the attitude of the British government to micro-electronics, though it taught little about the

THE AFFECTIVE DOMAIN	1 a Attitudes, values, beliefs b Affective skills (persistence, flexibility, attention to details, etc.)
THE COGNITIVE DOMAIN	2 a Factual knowledge b Understanding (eg explanation)

THE DOMAIN OF SKILLS	3 Intellectual skills
	   a Particular skills (eg calculus, programming, reasoning)
	   b Analytical skills (eg scientific, historical)
	   c Synthesis (eg design, creative writing, problem solving)

	4 Manual skills (eg typing, workshop)

devices themselves. Or again, employers are often inclined to say about new graduate recruits that 'attitude is everything'. The affective domain is an extremely important field of learning, but one which is hardly tackled consciously by universities. Nevertheless the three years at a campus university do a great deal to impart middle-class mores and attitudes to students as well as a belief in the academic approach to knowledge.

It is however clear that wrong expectations of a learning system by students can give rise to serious problems, and that this is one important aspect of the difficulties that students meet in making the transition from school to university life. It follows that in introductory or foundation courses, teaching methods, personal guidance and the social environment should be designed to smooth this transition.

Factual Knowledge and Understanding A simple fact for one person may be very abstruse for another. The facts of a balance sheet may be immediately grasped and remembered by an accountant, but may be quite incomprehensible and unmemorable for someone with no understanding of number or of the terminology and conventions that accountants use. Thus, understanding at some level — even if it is of the meanings of everyday words, let alone jargon — must precede the learning of facts.

The distinction is particularly important in continuing education.

A long undergraduate education in medical understanding is an essential prerequisite for a factual course in professional medical updating. Undergraduate courses ought in general to be concerned primarily with teaching understanding — supported, of course, with a good deal of factual information. Understanding usually takes a long time to teach well, but, given the understanding, factual knowledge can be rapidly and easily taught to interested students.

From this it follows that teachers of courses even of a factual nature must pay particular attention to their students' prior understanding. This is again a matter of particular importance in designing courses for students who have just entered an institution.

Intellectual Skills Intellectual skills are concerned with techniques and methods. Methods tend to require more insight than techniques. Thus it is possible, for example, for someone to have mathematics skills (addition, equation solving, differentiation) with no understanding. Such a person would be said to have been *trained* in mathematical *techniques.* On the other hand, using mathematical methods to solve a problem requires more than mere techniques. Learning to do so effectively is both an education and a training. It is possible to gain understanding without developing intellectual skills, but in general the two have to be intermixed to be of use. Indeed skill in certain kinds of analysis is an essential component of most forms of understanding.

Two particular kinds of intellectual skills are those of *analysis* (the breaking down of a complex problem into manageable parts) and *synthesis* (the putting together of manageable parts in order to achieve a new complex whole). Universities are mainly concerned with analytical skills (as well as with knowledge and understanding, of course) and spend a good deal of time on identifying their preferred analytical concepts. (The very activity, indeed, with which this section of this chapter is concerned.) Synthesis skills are taught and practised in universities to a much lesser extent than analytical ones, even in such fields as engineering, where creative design is a key skill. Also in English or art, criticism rather than creative writing or painting, say, is given pride of place.

Manual Skills Manual skills, even typing for computer keyboard operation, are taught very little in universities, though perhaps they should be given more attention. They usually call for relatively little knowledge, understanding or intellectual skill and so are outside the normal range of abilities of most academic staff.

It is often said that the main purpose of higher education is to 'teach students to think', but the set of aims shows that this can mean many different things. Understanding, and all kinds of intellectual skill, require some thought, but the modes of thought vary widely from subject to subject. So the verb 'to think' must be used with caution in descriptions of educational aims.

Briefly, the differences in educational strategy needed for these aims are:

a To change attitudes or habits (the affective domain) strong emotional or social experiences are needed.
b Knowledge of facts can be taught by any appropriate technique to interested students, who already have adequate understanding.
c Understanding — or conceptual development — requires more than one method (eg lectures plus books, or texts plus TV or kits) and a well structured feedback loop. (Concepts relate both to a content and to a variety of contexts; they must be used in a variety of exercises if they are to be understood.)
d Skills require instruction and practice under supervision. Intellectual skills (such as writing and mathematics) can be exercised with a fairly long feedback path (for error correction and encouragement), though the shorter the better. Practical skills are best dealt with in a face-to-face situation.

Proposition 4. A Discussion of the Evidence from Students
In the design of teaching, the central focus should be to stimulate, guide and support the individual student in his or her struggle to learn; from this it follows that

a Teachers should be aware of the strengths and limitations of different teaching methods, in relation to different educational aims. Even good lectures can only make a limited contribution, and where they are bad they must be changed or abandoned.
b Students must be assisted to guide and assess themselves by materials for individualized learning and for self-assessment.
c Projects, because of their ability to integrate different educational aims, and the strong motivation to learn they provide, should be widely used where they are appropriate.

Returning to the evidence presented earlier (pages 140 ff.), it is now clear that the students' comments are significant at a number of levels, but that the comments themselves do not necessarily distinguish between these levels. For example, a student may criticize a lecturer when the cause for criticism may well be that the educational aim is not really appropriate for a lecture (Interviews 2 and 6) or may praise him because he has operated more in the affective domain — and mostly communicated enthusiasm (Interview 5).

On the other hand several bad stories were characterized by self-doubt, by worry, by insecurity. They were characterized more by indifference or withdrawal than by hostility or anger (Interviews 2, 3, 4). The student's tendency, if one can take it from these stories, is not to shout, scream or protest, but simply to put a distance between himself and the situation he finds unpleasant. The good stories on the other hand are characterized by increased interest, by involvement in the subject, by a personal response to the teacher and by a desire to learn more: 'I wanted to work more because I felt I could' is a typical statement.

But the self-doubt could well be misdirected if, as seems likely, it arises from false expectations. The lecture is not normally a method in which the feedback loop is closed. It is primarily one in which the student is passive, and except for the most able students (who require no extra help) the communication is one-way, from teacher to student. Consequently, it is best used for educational aims which do not need the active participation of students in the conversational process. It is therefore good for:

a Conveying factual knowledge.
b Giving an extended, explanatory account of what has to be learned.
c Pacing students' studies.
d Demonstrating physical phenomena or methods of argument and presentation.
e Communicating enthusiasm and so, hopefully, changing students' attitudes and even values (the affective domain).
f Updating information.

It is weak in teaching conceptual development and in exercising intellectual skills. Many students' accounts make this clear; the following quotation illustrates the point.

'Um, well I would like to say that I think I learn most by working by myself, perhaps a few weeks before the exams. Um, well I take my notes and a couple of textbooks relevant to it. Sit down with lots of sheets of empty paper and just work through and sort of connect each equation with every other one, make sure it's all unified. Then if I can do this that brings the enjoyment again, you see, and keenness this sort of makes you want to carry on.'

Various choices, say between lecture courses and individualized learning with written study guides, can then be seen differently. They are not opposed opposites. The issue is how best to combine the live performance, with books and other resources that exist and with ad hoc material that could be written, in order to stimulate and sustain that active struggle, whether on one's own or in discussion, that is essential to learning. So the lecturer's target is not to become a better performer (although for all to do so would be a considerable advance) but to see and plan his contribution as part of a broader strategy to promote learning. Materials whereby students can assess themselves and sort out their own problems would be one essential component of such a strategy.

If it is one of the main aims of a course to develop the student's capacity to take responsibility for his own learning the lecture clearly has a role to play, but it is not that of effective teaching.

The evidence about tutorials (in science) illustrates all too clearly that the setting up of a small group teaching session, without first establishing whether its function is educationally viable, even though it offers close face-to-face contact between student and teacher, can be both stressful and ineffective. Evidently, tutorials must not only provide proper conversational learning (nor merely remedial tuition) but must also be handled sympathetically at a personal level. This may for example involve much more frequent meetings. Or again it could well be that remedial tuition should always be on a one-to-one basis between teacher and student rather than in a group. The most unsatisfactory beginning for tutorials, yet the most common, is the question, 'Have you any problems?' There are many ways of structuring the use of tutorials which do *not* seem to throw up this initial kiss-of-death question, yet in many universities they are neither used nor looked for.

Finally, the popularity with students of various types of project work ought to be noted; such work can include investigational, design, problem solving, and creative projects. This popularity alone argues for their use, but it arises at least in part because of the evident sense that such activities make to students and the full development of their powers that they evoke. A good project will involve, as well as develop, each one of the eight educational aims referred to earlier.

Proposition 5. Strategies for Students' Learning
Students should achieve a clear understanding of their aims, of the way in which each course is designed to meet these aims, and of the role of different teaching methods within the design. Such understanding should lead them to take more responsibility for their own learning and to take part in constructive criticism of courses.

These considerations about students point to more fundamental issues. Some of these emerge from studies of student perceptions which have differed in focus from that of the HELP study quoted above. For example, the studies of Abercrombie (1960) with medical and education students and of Madge and Weinberger (1973) with arts students both show that in courses with a professional orientation new features emerge because students' perceptions of the professions, and the shadows that these cast on their studies, become important.

W.G. Perry's study (1970) attempted to map the intellectual and ethical development of college students over the four years of their course. His analysis of interview results led to a developmental scheme describing the progress of students from simple polarities (all answers are either right or wrong, all actions good or bad, the right authority knows which is which), through stages of confusion (they know *the* answer but their game is to make us find what they could so easily tell us), to more mature stages in which the contextual and relative nature of knowledge and values are grasped, until finally the need for commitment to express one's identity is appreciated. Progress through these stages is not uniform and students temporize, escape or retreat in various ways because the changes they are called on to make lead to insecurity that they cannot bear. The one lecture or tutorial group may contain students who are all at different stages in this progression.

At this point several lines of argument may be seen to converge. One suggests that students should understand the conversational learning process in which they should be engaged, be aware of the different kinds of aims which their courses contain, and start to form their own models of learning. Another suggests that if courses pay more attention to the students' development they may concentrate more on the 'process' aims of their subjects rather than on 'content' aims, and this shift may have to be made clear to students who may come with different expectations. A third argument is that students should be led to take responsibility for their own learning but that they can only do this if the system which sets the boundaries and targets for their work is designed to make that clear.

The convergence may lie in setting out for the students a set of meta-aims explaining that for full awareness and control as a learner you need to know:

— What you know and understand (or not).
— That you know or understand (or not).
— The relation of this achievement to the aim of the course.
— The aims and mechanisms of the learning system in which you are involved.
— The range and purpose of the methods available for learning.
— How you are using them.

Both Perry and HELP books report that students expressed both surprise and gratitude to the researchers for taking a serious interest in their perceptions of their work, often saying that they were the first staff to do so. So there could be a felt need for such a programme.

However, serious work on deeper aims is not to be undertaken lightly. Perry closes his book by emphasizing that a student who needs to abandon old certainties and to see himself differently may well need careful support, and Abercrombie points out that when a student comes to see the need for change in himself 'such a message could be so painful that it would be rejected.'

ACADEMIC STAFF AS PROFESSIONAL TEACHERS

Proposition 6. The Need
Staff should commit themselves to becoming professional teachers; this involves, inter alia, the need to maintain minimum acceptable standards in teaching.

Whilst it is an issue to be debated whether a set of meta-aims is helpful to students, there can be no doubt that a knowledge of the importance of feedback for some educational aims, and an appreciation of what these aims are, is essential for the academic staff.

Teaching at university includes two, or possibly three main components: teaching, research and some administration. But it is only the teaching role that concerns us here. Even so, due to the interconnectedness of all aspects of such a complex process as education, research and administrative activities are bound to have their effect on the teaching function — a matter discussed further on pages 163 ff.

One approach is to consider the perceptions and attitudes of academics. Perhaps this can only be attempted by reference to well-known novels, but a few stereotypes might be described for consideration. Some lecturers are hard-headed and almost cynical, concentrating on research for advancement and paying minimal attention to teaching. Some regard themselves as serious and knowledgeable about teaching, but think that long discussion, serious reading and even careful planning make little difference; the best solutions are easily discerned and then one can return to research. Some settle into teaching as part of a withdrawal or regression from commitment to research or other leadership; they exemplify the label 'only a teacher', and whilst being conscientious and often devoted to students take little serious intellectual interest either in their subject or in teaching and learning. This type often serves as a warning to the ambitious young, showing what comes of taking teaching too seriously. Finally there are a few with an intellectual commitment to teaching and these are either under strain to prove themselves through unusual and suspect activities, or to shoulder the burden of establishing some research reputation as well as attempting serious development or even research work in teaching.

The point of these imperfect vignettes is to draw attention to the variety of roles adopted within the one organization. How that variety will change with ageing staff, and how the pressures of contraction and redundancy will also shift or break the patterns, remains to be seen — the changes can hardly be small ones.

One route to the improvement of the teaching work of staff is the establishment of special units devoted to the task. This has worked only slowly and with a minority of staff and departments. Staff in those units are expected to achieve fundamental improvements with marginal powers, and their failure to perform this miracle is held against them. Those whose role is to counsel students achieve success with individual cases, but most students will define their role in relation to their teaching staff.

The teaching methods working party is another method which attempts to put responsibility for improvement in the collective hands of some of those involved. It too offers no smooth path to success. Recruiting staff to give time to it is rarely easy; recruiting the right staff harder still. Discussions in it soon reveal deep differences about almost every matter at almost every level, from the vital need for rigour as opposed to the need to consider students' views, reactions and problems, to differences about how, when and what to teach. Passionately held positions are struck and defended, at least for the duration of a meeting.

There is no prospect that deep and real differences can be explored and reconciled within the time-span available. Worse, behind the clash of argument there often lies a deep lethargy; a feeling that time could be better spent doing something useful, like research or even teaching. So the working party papers over the cracks, and in the name of academic freedom leaves it to the staff who will actually do the teaching to interpret things in their own way. The staff are left tolerably happy, except for having once more reinforced the feeling that it is impossible and disagreeable to talk about teaching. The students barely notice the difference.

Another approach is to look for research evidence that will tell one what to do. Those with first-hand experiences of opening their classes to the peripatetic educational researcher, who casts the teacher and class as experimental rats, rarely find that the research report based on observing their work, which reaches them long after, bears much relation to their world or its problems. So they hope nobody will act upon it. Where such reports follow the genre of comparing this method with that ('surely we can show which way is better'), the experienced reader will remember the depressing review of Dubin and Taveggia (1968) which shows that almost all such work yields no significant differences. Perhaps the changes don't matter, or equally embarrassing, perhaps 'it all depends', so that one's own local versions of old or new methods cannot be guided by results obtained elsewhere (indeed if this were not true would not one be reduced to the experimental rat?).

One reason for these difficulties is that to take to one's heart approaches very different from those experienced or operated in the past requires a rather deep personal re-orientation. Those who have to train graduates for teaching know that even in a situation where the trainer's expertise is acknowledged and the criteria for competent professional performances are well defined, the trainee often finds that the reorientations required to find a new role are confusing, disturbing and painful.

Some types of teaching innovation expose this problem in a particularly sharp form. Certain types of project work, for example, put the teacher into the position of consultant where he does not know the answers and must admit to students that he cannot meet their expectations. Then the only choice is either to give way to anarchy or to develop a role which promotes creativity and responsibility amongst one's students whilst helping them as well as oneself to tolerate the uncertainty of the situation.

The main conclusion from this rather depressing sketch of academic teaching seems to be that nothing can be done to improve things. It is our view, however, that this is too harsh a conclusion. Evidence of the kind illustrated earlier shows that a deeper understanding of student learning difficulties and personal problems can be obtained and used. The growth of distance teaching in recent years has thrown into relief the need to understand the different roles that different teaching methods can play. Face-to-face teaching, in lectures, laboratories, and tutorials, as well as the many distance-teaching techniques, referred to later in this paper, all have their strengths and weaknesses, and it must now be a part of the professionalism of university teachers to be aware of these differences and to make proper use of this knowledge. This point is further developed on pages 160 ff.

However, it is also suggested here that deep matters of self-regard and personal orientation bear directly on the possibilities for change. But it does not follow that all action to this end must be private and lonely. Indeed, the privacy of much teaching creates many of the fears and fantasies, and inhibits the flow of mutual support and criticism which the same staff experience as essential in their research. One experienced advantage of Keller Plan and related schemes for individualized learning has been that the teachers' action is on paper, open for criticism and discussion. More generally a better developed corporate system, which could provide support stimulus and recognition, could be of key importance, and this raises the larger issue of professionalism in teaching.

Most of the recognized professions could scarcely tolerate the low level of competence that the below-average teacher displays in higher education. Lecturers ought to have more collective pride, be more ambitious and jealous for the good name of their work. A virtue of professionalism is that it sets up criteria and system pressures to help individuals to recognize themselves differently and so set themselves different targets. Enhanced co-operation and communication would be an inevitable part of a more jealous professionalism.

Successful professionals tend to achieve their status through a general acknowledgement by the public that a professional is the one most likely to give the service that is being looked for (eg doctors, solicitors). It is this kind of professionalism that should be offered in higher education.

Proposition 7. Characteristics of Professional Teaching
Professionalism in teaching in higher education implies

　a　More public exposure and discussion of teaching performance, course design and teaching materials.
　b　High scholarly status given within a discipline to the design and delivery of good teaching in that discipline.
　c　Use of appropriate models and strategies for the 'engineering' of teaching.

The concept of 'professional' is being used here in a special way. The meaning which the concept should acquire for this context is best illustrated by sketching out some of the features that would characterize professionalism for teachers in higher education.

The first relates to the suggestion of minimum standards: that idea cannot be implemented unless there is more public exposure of teaching, not only of teaching performance but also of course design and of the preparation of materials for students. Such exposure to critical discussion by peers and students is also an essential step towards raising the level of discourse amongst teachers about their work.

A second characteristic ought to be the recognition that the achievement of good teaching — which is to select a limited set of insights and aims and to express them at a limited level of sophistication in order to achieve the best, most authentic communication of the structure and spirit of a discipline — ought to be a challenge to the powers of any teacher. This challenge should be continually renewed, given that the scholar's own perspective on his subject is altered by experience of teaching and research. If the challenge is not keenly felt, it may be a sign that the teaching lacks scholarly ambition, a lack which, paradoxically, is more likely to produce courses incomprehensible to students than those based directly on the teacher's live concerns. Too much discussion about teaching methods overlooks the delicate interaction between them and the need to re-examine the deep structure of the subject matter. Too little discussion can overlook the need to teach effectively those who find it difficult to learn.

A third characteristic is that the design of a teaching activity is a 'problem-solving' task, more akin to engineering than to a science or an art. Engineers, like teachers, try to satisfy customers, usually using imperfect knowledge of many of the fundamental issues involved, and relying a good deal on experience. It is recognized that good engineers work by a judicious blend of theory, expressed in valid but simplified models, and a successful working scheme, integrated by experience and understanding of the workings of complex processes. Some such paradigm is needed for the teaching task. Warren Piper (1975) has expressed this as (a) being able to perceive significant aspects of the situations which confront him and to use theory to see, and select from, the possible courses of action and (b) possessing the necessary skills to act effectively upon such a choice. The models described earlier can contribute to the professional teacher's understanding and the list of methods given later indicates the range of skills need for this enterprise.

Proposition 8. Support for Developing Professional Teaching
The main responsibility for improving teaching within a discipline must belong to scholars in that discipline; experts in teaching methods can support and advise, whilst those equipped for research into teaching and learning should devote some of their resources to research commissioned by teachers.

As argued in Proposition 7 above, the structure and epistemology of a subject must be one of the main factors in determining the best means of promoting the learning of that subject. It follows that developments can only proceed by giving stimulus and support to subject experts. Experts in teaching and learning methods can provide them with tools for the job but they must not claim, or appear to claim, to have a single answer to the problems of teaching all subjects.

Similar remarks apply to research into teaching and learning. Academics clearly have the right to refuse to engage in research into teaching but they cannot refuse to be involved in the engineering of teaching. Difficulties often arise because this distinction is blurred. If it were made sharper, then it might be possible to consider whether some (not all) research into teaching and learning could usefully be looked at in the light of a 'customer-contract' principle, in which teaching developments define research needs. For the customer-contract principle to work well, the customer has to be clear about his own role as the responsible engineer and has to think out his own needs through his own struggles with his problems. The need for more 'research' in the area thus takes second place to the need to develop the professional conscience and consciousness of university teachers.

Propostion 9. Using Tools
Staff ought to know about the wide range of teaching methods now available; they should be able to select those methods which are most effective for the aims and contexts of the learning. In particular, most staff need to learn more about the professional skills needed for independent study and distance-learning methods.

An inescapable element of the engineering of teaching is the ability to use the tools of teaching effectively and skilfully. We have already discussed how educational processes and aims can be described; the problems of using them in practical teaching environments remain.

Until recently teaching was achieved either by correspondence, or face-to-face in lectures, small groups, laboratories, or on the job. Nowadays with the growth of communications technology of one kind or another, from computers to satellites and from telephone conferencing to television, teaching at a distance has grown greatly in sophistication and success, so much so that it is now sensible to consider augmenting face-to-face teaching with certain distance-teaching techniques (radio and TV have been used in school classrooms for many years) and vice-versa (as in the Open University).

It should, in addition, be accepted that distance-teaching techniques such as TV, radio or computer-aided methods will in general adopt different styles depending on whether they are intended to be audio-visual *support* for a teacher, or whether they are intended to stand alone.

The problem has become one of choosing the best technique for the particular educational task in hand. The techniques all differ as to cost, level of technological sophistication, educational effectiveness relative to aims, demands on teacher time, and so on; so the choice between them is not easy. The scale of the problem can be illustrated by the following list of the main methods available. This list is not meant to be complete or exhaustive and it is not of course suggested that a teacher should become expert in every one of the methods listed.

- a *Face-to-face* (including audio-visual aids)
    - i Lectures.
    - ii Classes (as in schools).
    - iii Small group discussions, usually for remedial purposes.
    - iv Tutorials (ie a teacher with no more than 3 students).
    - v Self-help groups (ie small groups without a teacher).
    - vi Laboratory or practical work (see g below).
    - vii The telephone and telephone conferencing.
- b *Printed texts*
    - i Text books.
    - ii Structured tutor-texts (as used in the Open University).
- c *Films or TV programmes*
    - i For broadcasting (ie *not* for repeated replay).
    - ii Films or TV tapes for repeated replay.

  Note: The replay facility, which at present is expensive because of the cost of the replay device, should strongly affect the content of such films or tapes for *some* educational purposes. Interactive video — that is programmed instruction attached to a video-disc — seems (unfortunately) to be on its way.
- d *Audio*
    - i For radio broadcasting.
    - ii Tapes (either delivered to students or accessed by telephone).
    - iii Audio-vision (ie audiotapes supported by printed illustrations, diagrams, calculations, etc.).
    - iv Telephone conferencing.
- e *Audio-graphic systems* such as Cyclops (ie the recording on audio-tape of both spoken commentary and of graphic or alphanumeric data for display on a TV screen).
- f *Computer-aided learning* (*CAL*)
    - i Using teletype terminals.
    - ii Using visual display units; such methods include Prestel, Optel and similar systems.
    - iii Using the mail (for distance teaching) and a word-processor for preparing the communication from the computer.
- g *Laboratory or practical work*
    - i In purpose-built teaching laboratories.
    - ii Based on practical apparatus for use in the home or at work.

iii Projects.
h *Assignments*
These can be associated with any of the above, but except in the case of CAL or tutoring they require the use of a further channel of communication.

It hardly needs to be pointed out that for any of these methods to be used good technology, from a clean blackboard to a video-disc with a good user software system, is essential.

The proper use of these methods, whether in a mainly face-to-face teaching establishment or in a mainly distance-teaching one is, or should be, what distinguishes a professional teacher. Too often a new method is 'tried out' on quite inappropriate material or to achieve aims to which it is clearly unsuited. We have seen earlier (pages 147 ff.) how the feedback model was able to bring to light some of the reasons for students' dissatisfaction with lectures and tutorials, and how the drawing of distinctions between different educational aims can guide the purposes for which lectures can be used more effectively. The same kind of insights can similarly inform the choice between other methods, though a good deal of research is still needed to bring these characteristics to light.

Television, for example, is essentially a means of communicating from teacher to student; it is a 'forward path' component of the learning loop and so, for conceptual development and for skills, it needs to be supported by a feedback communication path. Given such support it is an extremely powerful medium for 'instruction' and for demonstration. On its own, without support, it can be very effective in the affective domain and also of course, for its most commonly used educational application, that of presenting facts to students.

More generally, it should be noted that most staff in campus institutions have little familiarity with distance learning or individual study methods. Yet in the future more emphasis on continuing education and development of the role of institutions in helping part-time students will call for skilled selection and use of such methods.

Similar reasoning lies behind the optimum deployment of each method, but it must not be forgotten that matching educational methods to educational aims is only a small part of the professional teacher's task. Any method can be unsatisfactory for a variety of reasons. For example, it is likely to be relatively ineffective if:

a It is not provided with appropriate interaction between staff and students in fields where conversational learning is important.
b It is not matched to the educational aims.
c It is not suitable for the subject matter (eg chemistry, history, etc.).
d It does not adequately deal with some particular student's personal or learning needs.

e It does not attract the support and dedication of the teachers who use it.
f It costs too much.

EDUCATIONAL SYSTEMS

Proposition 10. Supporting Professional Development
Institutions should accept the need to define professional standards in teaching and should develop structures to stimulate and support staff in meeting such standards. This means that they must actively support the professional development of staff as teachers, including the learning of new skills and the development and use of methods to assess teaching work.

In educational institutions there are many interests other than teaching, and those responsible for policy may give higher priority to other concerns. Such matters as income and maintenance grants, administration and research, promotion and career prospects, may well divert time and effort from educational matters, and it is against such a background that improvements in teaching have to be brought about. Indeed until teaching ability becomes a stronger factor in the assessment of academics for promotion there may be little incentive for them to strive for improvement.

However, assessing educational expertise is by no means a simple matter, especially since there are few accepted criteria of good teaching. The least popular lecturer, for example, may make the greatest impact on students. Furthermore, teaching and lecturing are very personal matters, and the presence of an academic colleague in a lecture as an observer can be very distressing for some. There is not space here to do justice to the problem of the evaluation of teaching but a few general points can be offered. The preparation of teaching texts, whether by individuals or, as in the Open University, by course teams, exposes each author to the criticism of his colleagues, and some find such criticism very hard to take, especially at the beginning. Indeed it is common for academics to try to cling to their manuscripts until it is too close to a production deadline for comments to be made. Somehow exposure to students and to the world seems more bearable than the comments of colleagues! Overcoming this sensitivity to criticism, or merely to observation in a lecture, is undoubtedly a key step towards achieving improvements and towards genuine professionalism. For example, it should become normal practice, as already is the case in some universities, for staff to attend each other's lectures or tutorials, and so to learn good practice from each other. A system of mutual evaluation of this type is described by Mathias and Rutherford (1982).

It must not be forgotten that there are cogent arguments that can be advanced against taking a more professional approach to teaching, and the weight that individual academics give to them is often more a matter of value judgement and attitude than of reason and evidence. It is held by many, for example, that the universities' role is primarily one of research and of pushing back the frontiers of knowledge, and that the best education for students is to be close to, and listen to, those who are engaged in such work. For the brightest students, whose future also lies in research, there is much strength in this argument, but, for the majority of students such an apprenticeship to research is hardly suitable. Allied to this is the view that it is not the task of universities, even if it is the aim of the polytechnics, to prepare people for professional work. This is sometimes even held to be the case in engineering departments, though it has not yet gained much strength in medical or dental schools.

Again it can be argued that if students are to be taught to 'think', defined here as the ability to seek out knowledge for themselves, then effective teaching, and even a supportive environment may not be the best preparation. However, those with experience of the most problem-oriented and project-based education know that these lead to demands from students for effective teaching, both of specific areas of understanding and of particular skills, so that serious attention to such work demands more rather than less of the skills and commitment of teachers. Open-learning systems, in which students are not full-time on a campus or are not put on prescribed courses, may be a much cheaper way of achieving such education, particularly nowadays with so many home-based learning systems available, but they can only be effective if they are prepared with care and professional skill.

Proposition 11. Taking Decisions about Changes in Teaching
Institutional systems for consultation, for making decisions and for delegating authority should be consonant with the needs and rights of staff in teaching, whether as individuals or as course teams.

The structure of authority in most institutions does not make it easy to bring about change, even of so simple a nature as improved mutual interaction amongst those teaching the same course. It is not simply a matter of carrying through the right policy decisions. For example in polytechnics, where directorates tend to have more authority than pro-vice-chancellors and deans, there are particular problems. Unlike senior academics in universities, the senior staff in polytechnics do not as a rule take part themselves in the task of teaching students, with the inevitable result that for them administrative problems loom larger than teaching ones.

Imposition from above is a well-known way of ruining a good idea. Few heads of department fall into this trap: many, having been on the receiving end in the past, go too far to escape it, thereby exercising no leadership. Imposition may fail because academics are prone to be prima donnas, or more frequently because turning policy into action in education is far from trivial because innovations have to evolve through experience, which often means that policy made from above cannot work. Aim and action are not neatly related as premises and conclusions in logic, and where action may transmute aims or expose new ones, the executor has to be in authority.

So the only alternative to leaving all to do their own thing individually is some form of collective process which challenges and supports individuals and sub-groups and which, whilst respecting the freedom and authority within their teaching that they must have with their students, works also to make the members take some responsibility for the overall co-ordination of the students' learning.

Thus just as a particular innovation, such as project work, can disturb the location and nature of power and authority between staff and student, so any move to fundamental reform of teaching may need or even give rise to changes in the authority, distribution of power and relationships within a staff group. That is to say, changes may have political implications. (By the same arguments, any serious attempts to involve learning more closely with the needs of society may lead to a shift to give more direct power to society in forming university academic policy, as has happened for example in Sweden.)

Proposition 12. The Best Use of Resources
Staff should be aware of the relative costs per student hour of various methods, should bear these in mind in designing courses and should pursue collaboration with other institutions for the sharing of resources and materials wherever possible.

Questions of costs, or preferably cost-effectiveness, do not always argue in favour of the use of new teaching methods, though they obviously argue in favour of a more effective use of existing methods. A useful parameter by means of which to begin a study of costs, in both human and financial terms, is the number of academic hours required to produce one student hour of work. Dividing this parameter by the number of students taught gives an overall measure of staff time and effort and cost per student taught. The following are approximate representative figures (see p. 166).

Other factors affect the costs, such as capital costs and the number of support staff involved in preparing the teaching material (eg in TV) and the proportion of the teachers' salaried time spent on teaching (eg only about 10 per cent in many cases).

It is clear from these figures that non face-to-face methods require a good deal of investment of time and money and for them to be cost-effective they need substantial student audiences. Unless such large audiences are to be found, face-to-face methods are in general the least expensive. But unless each method is matched to the intended educational aims and is embedded in an appropriate educational system it is unlikely

	Academic hours per student hour	Typical numbers of students
Lecturing	1 - 2	50
Small group classes	1 - 2	15
Audio-vision	10 - 20	5000
TV (tapes or broadcast)	5 - 100	100s - 1000s
Multi-media teaching (including TV and text)	50 - 80	5000
CAL	100 - 200	1000

to be cost-effective however cheap it is. If high technology methods (such as TV, CAL, video-disc, etc.) are to be used in conventional universities they can only engage sufficient student numbers if they are used on several cohorts of students — either in several collaborating universities or over a number of years, or both. Many academic subjects, however, seem to lend themselves to precisely this kind of treatment so that much is to be gained from such collaboration.

Also, as indicated in the table, particularly with television, it is possible to produce some kinds of educational material (eg recorded lectures for video-tape replay) which are very inexpensive. These can become cost-effective in appropriate fields with quite small student numbers, and so can be used as pilots for more ambitious collaborative schemes which might have to be developed to realize the full potential of some methods.

Proposition 13. Supporting Innovations
Innovations in teaching need particular support and protection if they are to develop their full potential and if the staff involved are to have a fair reward for the risks that they take.

A great deal more might be said about the style of work required to generate changes in teaching and learning. The account of inter-university collaboration of physicists in the HELP project (Black and Ogborn 1977) bears on this issue. The need for long discussion, for tolerating uncertainty about new developments, for allowing individual variants to be carried through, for the mutual confidence needed to establish open inspection and assessment of one's day's work, are all relevant features that arose in the work there described. It should also be recognized that teaching innovations require particular support, since a teaching idea often needs a great deal of adaptation before it can meet its aims, or even before it can become clear which aims it has the potential to serve.

There are many ways to support such innovations. The central ones are to increase teachers' knowledge of the teaching and learning processes, to establish the impetus towards professionalism, and to build up ways of mutual working by which staff can support one another in coping with the intellectual and personal pressures that a serious attempt to do better must generate. Experts in 'teaching' can give only limited help; a heightened awareness in each teacher is essential.

Two indirect ways to support such innovations lie in further researches firmly grounded in practice, and styles and channels of publication that express and establish the academic presence of the work, whilst speaking at a level and in a style that can ensure reception and use by peers. To talk briefly about these approaches is not to imply that the problems of innovation are small or that they have been solved at all in the past.

REFERENCES

Abercrombie, M.L.J. (1960) *The Anatomy of Judgement* London: Hutchinson

Black, P.J. and Ogborn, J. (1977) Inter-university collaboration in methods of teaching science *Studies in Higher Education* 2 (2)

Bliss, J. and Ogborn, J. (1977) *Students' Reactions to Undergraduate Science* London: Heinemann

Bridge, W. and Elton, L. (1977) *Individual Study in Undergraduate Science* London: Heinemann

Dubin, R. and Taveggia, T.C. (1968) *The Teaching-Learning Paradox* University of Oregon at Eugene: Center for the Advanced Study of Educational Administration

Madge, C. and Weinberger, B. (1973) *Art Students Observed* London: Faber

Mathias, H. and Rutherford, D. (1982) Lecturers as educators: the Birmingham experience *Studies in Higher Education* 7 (1) 47—56

Ogborn, J. (1977a) *Small Group Teaching in Undergraduate Science* London: Heinemann

Ogborn, J. (1977b) *Practical Work in Undergraduate Science* London: Heinemann

Pask, G. (1976) *Consersation Theory* Amsterdam: Elsevier

Perry, G. (1970) *Forms of Intellectual and Ethical Development in the College Years* New York: Holt, Rinehart,, Winston

Warren Piper, D. (1975) *The Longer Reach in Issues of Staff Development* London: UTMU